Under The Mosquito Net

An Inside Look at Missions

Ron Smith

Dr. Ron Smith participated on a team of 6 translators, successfully translating the New Testament into the tribal dialect of former headhunters in Northeastern India. As well, Ron and his wife Judy, together with another friend, were co-founders of the School of Biblical Studies in Youth with a Mission. Since 1981, more than 300 of these schools have been offered on every inhabited continent. Both Ron and Judy have graduate degrees in divinity and theology. Ron has written 3 books, contributed articles in 2 others as well as contributions in Christian journals and magazines. In the last 23 years, Dr. Smith has preached in 45 countries and trained other missionaries from all over the world. He lives in Lakeside, Montana with Judy, his wife of 27 years.

To Sam Wilson
(Somewhere in the Middle East)

To the memory of Betty Wilson
(Somewhere in Heaven)

Maybe you've heard the term "benchwarmer."

Maybe you've even thought of that in relation to a pew, just holding down your spot and keeping it warm, Sunday after Sunday.

As for missionaries, however, they tend to be a little different — and their stories do, too.

This is a book of missionary stories. Some of them are my own, and some from people I've known and loved through the years. Some are funny, some are poignant. And some, like the one you're about to read, have to do with pews.

Not long after my friend Sam graduated from Baylor University in the 1960's, the Lord called him and his wife, Betty, to Mexico to spread the gospel.

It was a quick call, apparently: God spoke to them one day, and on the next, they found themselves packing up their Mercedes-Benz station wagon and heading south.

Well, during Sam's ministry there, he went to straighten out a church high atop a mountain south of Mexico City. Unfortunately, Sam was not offered lodging for his one-week stay. Looking for accommodations on his own, he found an old, abandoned Catholic church at the bottom of the mountain. The old building sported no doors, no windows and no roof — but it did have pews, and Sam saw them as a place to sleep.

As the night dragged on, the frosty wind whipped through the abandoned structure. In the pitch black, Sam lay and shivered on the old wooden pew. At one point, he noticed that the pew shook even when he stopped, and much to his surprise, he saw that there was another man sleeping at the other end.

Sam called out in Spanish, "What are you doing here?" The figure sat up and responded, "I am a missionary." Next, Sam asked him, "How do you stay warm here?"

The other missionary promptly displayed a newspaper page and tore it in half, giving half of it to Sam. "Take this and use it for cover, and pray to God that the morning comes."

When Sam told me this story, God captured my heart for missions forever. That day, I learned in a new way what discipleship really meant. I thought to myself, "So this is the price some people around the world pay in order to teach the truth."

From that time on I wanted to be like Sam, who just wanted to be like Jesus.

Today Sam has gone to the middle east. Betty Wilson has gone to heaven.

And, as for me? I've never looked at a pew the same way again.

ACKNOWLEDGEMENTS

This book is really the fulfillment of a dream. God called me to missions through hearing a story of pain and sacrifice. First, I acknowledge the Lord who spoke to me through my friend and professor in College, Dr. Sam Wilson. Everyone does not have this same experience in a calling. Second, I want to thank Fiona Soltes for her excellent editing and re-write of many of my clumsy statements. Third, I want to thank all of our faithful financial supporters through the years, without whom, there would be no ministry and thus no book. Fourth, I want to thank Kerry Neve and Kay Lindley for praying this thing through. Fifth, thanks to my wife, Judy, for her ongoing encouragement that this book needed to be published. Sixth, thanks to Mark Neubauer for the creative cover art. Finally, thanks to Mission Builders International for creating the platform for launching this book.

TABLE OF CONTENTS

Introduction 11

Chapter One 17
  Missionary Cuisine
  Taste and See that the Lord is Good

Chapter Two 27
  Missionary Money
  The Check's in the Mail

Chapter Three 47
  Personal Problems Among Missionaries
  Are You There, God? It's Me, Your Missionary

Chapter Four 75
  Missionary Failures

Chapter Five 90
  Missionary Successes

Chapter Six 104
  Missionary Pain

Chapter Seven 130
  Follow Their Example
  Following the Leader or What Part of "Yes"
  Do We Not Understand?

Conclusion 138
  How to Get Involved in Missions

Epilogue 142
  From Mission Builders International

AN OPENING WORD

FROM DANNY LEHMANN

"One of the common characteristics that I have found among 21st century young people with whom I work is their shared disdain for anything phony and their common appreciation for authenticity. Whether it's in the Latin American, African, Asian, or the Western worlds, most folks in this generation will listen to anything you have to say, as long as you say it 'straight-up!'

Ron Smith has done us all a favor by giving us an inside look at 'missions-straight-up.' Pulling no punches, he addresses hard-core issues and realities that missionaries face every day on the field—such as temptations to lust, depression, and the nagging sense of failure that plague many who have taken up Jesus' command to GO.

Two things qualify Ron to write on the subject of missions. First, he has been in the trenches doing it for the last 20-plus years. Secondly, he is well read enough in the disciplines of Theology, History, and Missiology to know what he's talking about!

Although *Under the Mosquito Net* has enough of what some would call the negative side of missions to smack the reader in the face with reality, it also has enough of the ultimate triumph of the One who called us to go and glorious success stories to keep our hearts full of hope that Jesus is ultimately victorious, even through what we might consider failure.

This generation has been called 'extreme' and always seems to be up to the latest challenge. If you are up for a challenge then this book is for you. There is none greater than the one Jesus gave us, 'Go and make disciples of all nations.' Read carefully, prayerfully and obediently."

Danny Lehmann

(Host for "Word to the World" radio program heard on over 400 stations nation-wide)

Director, Youth With A Mission, Hawaii

INTRODUCTION

I HOLD IN MY hand a directory for people interested
in short term missions involvement. It is a recently
published work that profiles most major ministries,
Bible Colleges, Seminaries and Short-term missions.
The pictures are glossy, the people are smiling and
over-all this is a very attractive piece of work. The
book is precise, it is attractive and makes missions
attractive. No doubt many people have been called to
missions for a short time and other people have been
called to a career in missions through that document
and others like it. I salute the many famous authors,
graphic designers and editors. That recruiting piece,
like the Bible could be termed a "Sharp two-edged
sword."

The book you hold in your hand is not a "sharp
two-edged sword." This book is a "blunt instrument." It
is raw, it is stark and it is frank. There are few
quotable phrases, few quotations of other popular
missions writers. In this book, you will read about
hungry missionaries, sexually tempted missionaries,
failed missionaries and successful missionaries. I
want you to read what I have read. I want you to hear
what I have heard, to see, to taste, to smell and men-
tally touch what I have heard, seen, tasted, smelled

and touched. The only way I know to make that happen is to tell the truth as honestly as I can without either making it uglier or prettier than it really has been.

As I write this introduction, I am in the middle of a three-day session of prayer and fasting for money with 25 missionaries. These missionaries are people like me, like you. Today we prayed for Dental bills to be paid, a new vehicle to be found, a school loan to be paid off, rent to be paid and monthly support to be increased. This is a picture of a missionary life in microcosm.

This book will surprise you. You may disagree with parts of it but please give me a fair hearing because this really is the way the world has been for me in the past twenty years. As you will read, many in other generations have experienced the same things, which I will describe for you. Some have experienced different principles for missionary endeavor and behavior. Nevertheless if you accept what I write as generally true for missionaries, you won't be far off.

As well, since this book has been ten years in the writing [literally on different continents and in different airplanes] some of the footnotes may not be as precise as any of us wish. The quotations and the statistics are [to the best of my knowledge] correct. Sometimes, a fact was so juicy that I just had to get it and in the excitement, I forgot to make a proper citation-for this I apologize. I also apologize to my former English and History professors who, if they are dead are rolling over in their graves and if they are living will want to claim no influence on my work. For this I confess and bewail my academic sins. I will try to give proper credit to whom it is due and to those I have overlooked, God is truly your reward.

Ron Smith
October 2002

Hannington, the first Anglican Bishop of Equatorial Africa, was murdered on his way inland from Mombasa, presumably on the order of Mwanga, King of Uganda in 1885.

A History of the Expansion of Christianity
Vol. 5, p.414
Kenneth Scott Latourette

"And you, take wheat and barley, beans and lentils, millet and spelt, and put them into a single vessel, and make bread of them. During the number of days that you lie upon your side, three hundred and ninety days, you shall eat it. And the food which you eat shall be by weight twenty shekels a day; once a day shall you eat it. And water you shall drink by measure, the sixth part of a hin; once a day you shall drink. And you shall eat it as a barley cake, baking it in their sight on human dung."

Ezekiel 4:9–12

CHAPTER ONE

Missionary Cuisine
or Taste And See That the Lord Is Good

THEY WERE WORDS that would silence the congregation.

"So, when was the last time you ate a dog?"

As a teacher of missionaries, I often hear—and love to repeat—tales of the "delicacies" of faraway lands. But this time was a little different. I was addressing not missionaries in training that day, but rather everyday churchgoers as part of a Swiss conference.

It was the Lord's idea, of course, that I even brought the dogs up. My wife and I had been living near Bern, Switzerland, back in 1987–88, and when a church a couple of hours away asked me to speak, I was at a loss for a subject. I had a one-sided conversation with God about it for some time, but still no answer.

Finally, it got to the point that I was actually on the train headed for the conference when the small, still voice filled me in: I was to share the most distasteful missionary stories imaginable.

Thus, the dogs. And more. Much, much more. But, we'll get to that in a minute.

First, take a moment and imagine yourself in that congregation. Maybe you're intrigued. Maybe, truth be told, you're a little squeamish. Or maybe you just don't believe it's true. I asked my Philippine friend, Rolo, one time if he had ever partaken, and smiling, he replied, "Only on special occasions. The last time I ate one was at my birthday party."

Friend, God speaks in mysterious ways. Though my stories were dreadful — and the feasts unimaginable — several people were called to the mission field that day. So, as you read the stories here, place yourself not only in the congregation, but also at that table; maybe there is a place set just for you, too.

So, open up wide and get ready to swallow.

Ever found a hair in your soup? In the case of my young friend, Jens, it was supposed to be there. Jens was hunting for an unreached migratory tribe in Indonesia, and when he found them, he preached the gospel to them for the first time in their history.

To thank him, the tribe held a special tribal dinner in his honor, and seated him next to the chief. A large pot boiled on a nearby fire, and finally, Jens' curiosity got the best of him. "What are we going to eat?" Just as he asked, two men walked toward the fire with a monkey draped over a bamboo pole, bound by its hands and feet. Nonchalantly, the chief grabbed the monkey by the nape of the neck, and threw it into the pot. Monkey soup — hair and all!

And then there was Leslyn, who worked with us on our Youth With A Mission staff in Hong Kong and other places throughout Asia. Just like Jens, Leslyn succeeded in reaching a difficult group for the gospel — and she received a feast of special culinary delights of her own. Following the meal, a small bird was produced. The bird's beak was promptly placed over the edge of a drinking vessel, and as Leslyn watched, the chief squeezed the bird's neck until saliva oozed out of its beak and into the vessel. Next, the saliva was mixed with another liquid, and the vessel began making its rounds. A toast, anyone, to the spread of the gospel?

Meanwhile, over in East Africa, my friend Martin was having a unique experience all his own. One night, following a meal of stuffed cow intestine, Martin was offered milk for dessert. He responded positively to the chief's offer, and before long, found himself faced with a cow in the banquet area. He assumed — correctly — that he'd have some warm milk for a treat. But he got a little more than he bargained for in his cup. After milking the cow, the tribesmen pulled out a knife and slashed open a wound directly behind the shoulder of the cow. The blood was then drained into the milk for just the right mixture, just for the honored guest.

Some cultures, believe it or not, delight in serving sex organs. Two friends of mine, Tom and Donna, traveled to West Africa to establish a Bible school. Once again, it was that farewell/thank you fest they had to look out for. The students decided to throw them a huge going away party, and one of the featured delicacies was goat testicles. This is paralleled only by the bull penis that was severed and served to some of my other missionary friends, who traveled through China as a basketball team. (Incidentally, my friends were billed in the area as the "NBA All-Start Team." An aspiring Chinese guy probably made a fortune on that one — but he probably missed out on the feast.)

As for me, I'm always up for a challenge. I'll admit, I don't like fish, but I've eaten a lot of it in my years on the mission field. One night, a Samoan student named Bob speared a large ocean fish for me, and cooked it up barbeque style. He was certain that if I tried it this way, I'd love it.

Well, as we bowed to pray, Bob placed that big old fish in front of me, face up, with its eye looking right at me. What could I do? I was not to be outdone, so, as we looked up from praying, I gouged that eye right out and ate it. And the fish really was delicious.

Not all experiences are so challenging, of course. Some are simply delightful. Anyone who has ever been to Singapore will know what I mean. According to one estimate, there are 980 restaurants listed in the yellow pages of their phone book — and that doesn't even touch the thousands of street vendors who offer marvelous food at marvelous prices. If you're truly blessed enough to eat in Singapore, you'll find food from everywhere in the world. On the list: Malaysian and Indonesian satay; Korean beef, called Bulgogi; and Indian Roti Pratah, which is like a Mexican tortilla with hot peanut and chili sauce on it. It's enough to keep anybody on the fields of Southeast Asia!

God has also been faithful to serve up lots of tasty stuff here in the United States. One night, when I was supposed to be flying to the city/nation of Singapore, I was "forced" by the airline to spend the night in a San Francisco Bay-area hotel. There, I found an exquisite restaurant overlooking a beautiful harbor. Since the airline had given enough meal vouchers to buy a multiple course buffet at the restaurant — and I had been told it was one of the preferred restaurants in the area — I went for it. And boy, was I glad I did. The food was an experience, but so was the clientele. I realized, while looking around me, that the others were in an income range that was certainly foreign to my own as a missionary — not to mention that of virtually everyone I knew.

The Proverbs tell us that, at times, there are "lizards in king's palaces." And oh, how I understood that idea that night, overlooking the beautiful bay.

Just as the Lord delights in sharing his feasts with us — no matter where we may be — some missionaries have the delight of sharing their own foods with others.

Bruce Olsen, for example, was used mightily to reach a tribe called the Motilones in South America. He traveled there when he was just 19 years old. In a role reversal, however, Olsen brought one of the leaders of the tribe back to the United States. He offered a meal of beef, but his guest balked at the thought of eating cow. His response? "If I can eat a grub worm, you can eat a cow." (And if you ever want to hear more about this hero of the faith's adventures, look for a book called *Bruchko*.)

Missionaries even find surprises in sharing with other Christians from different parts of the world. While I was in seminary, for example, I met a student from Germany named Wolfgang. He smuggled Bibles into Eastern European countries and the Soviet Union during the late 1960's and early 1970's. But, that's another story.

Wolfgang told me that in Germany it's not uncommon to see kegs of beer in the fellowship halls of Baptist churches, much as we'd see the coffee urns in our own halls here. Take away the coffee and donuts and bring in the pretzels and beer!

(But don't even think of judging our brothers and sisters there. Remember Romans 14 and 15?)

Through the years, even the most basic foods eaten by missionaries have had the potential to confuse the natives. When some of the earlier missionaries of the century traveled to the Congo, things got off to a good start. The natives enjoyed the missionaries, and cultivated a relationship with them. But, later on, the natives began pulling back. Confused by that behavior, one of the missionaries took it upon himself to ask an elder of the tribe what had happened. The old man related this story:

"When you came, you began to eat out of a can. You would open a tin can, which had a picture of corn on it, and corn would be inside and you would eat it. Then you would open a can, which had a picture of meat on it, and you would eat meat out of the can. You would open a can with a picture of fruit on it and you would eat fruit out of the can. Then, after you had your babies, you began eating out of cans with pictures of babies on them. This scared us."(*Customs and Cultures,* Eugene Nida)

No wonder!

His confusion was perfectly logical — just as mine was in the early 1990's my wife and I were with some Chinese folks in Taiwan. It was one of the most bizarre situations I've ever faced.

While there, my host, Don, walked into his living room with a half dozen "century old eggs" for us.

Believe it or not, these are duck eggs that have been marinated in horse urine for six months. When I held one of the eggs up to the light, it was so black that it resembled an onyx stone and not an egg at all.

When I tell this story, I'm often asked how they ever came up with the idea, and I can honestly say that I have no clue. But the most surprising thing — aside from the fact that I tried them — is that they really didn't taste bad, but they were really salty.

You know, as I look back over these "distasteful" stories, something else comes to mind. Unfortunately, it's even more distasteful, and it has not so much to do with food as much as it does lack of it.

Ever hear of Elisabeth Elliot? In addition to being the widow of slain missionary Jim Elliot, she wrote *A Chance to Die* the life of Amy Carmichael, who never took a furlough in all of her 52-year missionary career. In the story, Elliot mentions a missionary named Gardiner who worked in Latin American during the 1800's. He starved to death.

Granted, that's pretty hard for us to imagine if we've never faced it ourselves. In fact, we quote passages about God not letting the "righteous receive begging bread." No doubt, Gardiner knew that verse. But, he starved anyway. And he was not alone.

There was also the story of Lottie Moon, a great Baptist missionary from Virginia. If you yourself are a Baptist, you're probably familiar with the Lottie

Moon collections around Christmas every year. But, did you know that Lottie traveled to China without much support from her denomination or other Christians around her?

Anyway, after Lottie arrived in China, God began to pour out His Spirit in Lottie's ministry in powerful ways. There were many conversions, and many churches planted. Through it all, Lottie wrote letters back to America. She told of the triumphs, and she asked for Baptist pastors to come to China to lead the churches that had started as a result of her evangelism.

Lottie begged, pleaded and cajoled. The Presbyterians responded, and a few of the ministers went to oversee the Baptist churches. Lottie, bold as she was, took the opportunity to chide the totally male leadership of the Baptist conference overseeing Virginia that when God wanted to start Baptist churches in northeast China, he had to send not only a woman, but also Presbyterians.

To make a long story short, in the late 1800's, a terrible famine fell on northeast China where Lottie was ministering.

Once again, Lottie began sending letters to the Baptist saints in America. This time, she asked for food and money, because death was everywhere. And yet, she received little to no response.

Again, another letter, informing American churches that the money was urgent not only for food, but also for medical supplies.

And again, no response.

In desperation, Lottie began to withdraw her own money from an account she had established years earlier, just so the people could be fed. She withdrew her money again and again, until finally the account was empty.

Meanwhile, as the church in America continued to stand by without sending more money, Lottie fell ill herself.

She grew weaker and weaker, and though a hospital ship passing through the area took her in as a patient, she died on Christmas Eve, 1912 with starvation-related symptoms. In all honesty, the church in America let her die.

The Scriptures teach us in the book of 3 John that we do a loyal thing when we help the messengers of the gospel along their way. This passage is 2,000 years old, but the message is still fresh — especially when a messenger of God is helped and the forces of darkness are pushed back by well-equipped warriors for God.

Of course, for a warrior of God to fight, he must be fed.

CHAPTER TWO

Missionary Money
or The Check's in the Mail

"There are of course exceptions but, overall, giving among God's people, as the statistics show, is more or less a scandal."

George Verwer
Founder of "Operation Mobilization"
Out of the Comfort Zone p. 122

GOD CALLED ME to missions while I was in college, after listening to Sam's testimony. God fulfilled this call almost ten years later, asking Judy and me to step out of our pastorate in our small church in Massachusetts. I remember the situation vividly. While dropping the training application into the mailbox, I argued with God.

I told Him, "If Judy ever misses one meal because of this, I will come back to America and pastor a church with a board, a salary and security." God spoke clearly to me as I look back on it in hindsight.

He said, "If you will do this, I will take as good care of you in missions as I have in the pastorate." This has proved to be a large understatement on God's part. He has treated us like a king and queen since we came to the mission field in 1980. I do not remember missing a meal because of lack. We have, however, known what it means to be abased at times.

I remember being in the hot summer heat of Pusan, Korea in 1981. Judy and I prayed for money. We did not have one dollar. We prayed that God would send us one so that we could buy a coke, it was so hot. We received a letter from a friend named John Davidson who said he felt that God spoke to him to give us a $1 bill. We had a coke.

The apostle Paul knew how to be abased and how to abound. One dollar in an envelope comes under the abasing category.

As I travel around the world, one of the questions I commonly pose to my missionary friends is "How is your financial support?" Their answer is usually, "Inadequate"-by about 7 to 1. This answer comes at the rate of about 7 who answer "inadequate" to 1 of those who answer "adequate". In contrast to this — sharp contrast — I have never had one missionary tell me that he or she has "too much" support. This is after many years of asking.

What this means is that you can pretty well assume that the missionary you support needs more. This is true both for friends supporting individual missionaries and churches supporting individual missionaries.

The Bible highlights missionary support in the life of the apostle Paul. Philippians chapter 4 sheds light on his support structure. Paul writes that no church had entered into a regular support structure with him for a long time except for the Philippians. This reveals many things to us. First, the premier missionary in church history did not have an abundance of churches supporting him. This is important to understand. Famous missionaries with huge ministries and great responsibility are not over-supported. Many people with large ministries have only a few churches or individuals supporting them — if that many.

In Philippians 4, notice also that Paul says that he is not complaining of want. This is also consistent with missionaries I know. In Uganda, for example, I asked our national staff to bring their wallets to a staff meeting so we could pray over their wallets that God would fill them. Nathan, one of our national brothers, came to the meeting with nothing. He laughed a deep belly laugh and roared: "I don't have a wallet, what do I need a wallet for? I have no money!" Both his lack and his attitude are consistent with what I have found to be true all around the world. Paul, the apostle, wrote that he had faced both abundance and want in his career.

The apostle Paul had reasons to complain about support. He was constantly in motion. This motion was either in preaching and teaching or in running from persecution or getting caught and spending time in jail. Paul did not complain of want. He looked out for the spiritual well being of the church and thus looked for God to develop spiritual fruit in their lives based on both giving and receiving. Both the book of Acts and Philippians show us that.

The missionary money problem compounds as we consider the average giving of Christians around the world. Christians, worldwide, give an average of about 2% of their income to the work of God. All of this includes the pastor's salary, the church organ, the carpet and the missionaries. The U.S. Center for World Missions in Pasadena, California estimated recently that the average missionary needs $26,000 per year of committed support to function in a healthy way on the mission field. I know a few missionaries with that kind of income — very few.

One of the "under-supported many" is a friend of mine named Tammie. She looked up from her Mandarin lesson in downtown Taipei to say that her home church had been encouraging at times during her 10 years on the mission field in Asia. She smiled and said they had "sent her money" at times early on. For 3 years after that, though, she heard nothing from her home church.

When she finally did hear from them, the pastor

said that he was sorry that the church did not have the money to support her because they were in the process of building a new sanctuary. Most of her support has come from elsewhere, including another church that is not even her home church.

Paul's home church would probably be labeled in Antioch of Syria. We read nowhere that they supported him financially. They prayed for him and sent him off on his work but we do not read about money. As I said before, missionaries with large responsibilities are not over supported. Paul wrote in Philippians that "no church entered into partnership with me" except for the Philippians. Lack of home church support extends all the way back to the first century, all the way back to the apostle and theologian extraordinaire in the first century.

Speaking of home church support, my friend Don called me late one night from the Republic of China (Taiwan). He said that his church had split in the USA and now they told him that they could not support him among the Chinese because of the split. Suddenly they had no money. His church prayed for him but sent no money.

In ten years, Don and his family had never asked his church for money. During that same ten years, they had ministered, literally, all over the world. The pastoral answer to Don's letter of need was a photocopy of the pastor's letter of resignation to the church and a statement of empathetic understanding of Don's dire situation.

Don prayed and God showed him Mark chapter 6 about the apostles in the storm out on the lake. Jesus was sitting on the mountain watching. God knew there would be a storm. Confronted with commitment to his call, Don was asked a question by the Lord, "Are you willing to starve to death in obedience to My call?" Don pondered and finally answered, "Yes." Don knew the Lottie Moon story before he answered that question, by the way. Within a week or two a couple who had never sent money, sent $500 to Don and his family. Don presently runs a very dynamic work, which is affecting the Mandarin Chinese world as well.

Jesus preached that where our treasure is, there will our hearts be also. This is true for individuals, and it is also true for fellowships and churches.

The primary question in missionary support is "How much is missions worth to people? How important is reaching the whole world with the gospel of salvation — in terms of dollars?" Ultimately money shows us what we place our value on. Various cultures around the world value different things.

The missionary support question is really a "What do I value?" question.

Like the king's umbilical cord in Ugandan tradition (which is considered to be of great value), some churches place more value on their carpet than the lives of their missionaries. Several years back, I sat in a church and watched in horror as my wife wept. We were present as a church worshipped the "king's umbilical cord" — not literally in Uganda — but in America. Let me describe the scene to you.

Joe and Jane (not their real names) went to West Africa and both contracted malaria. This was in the middle of a school they were starting in a French speaking country that had very few Bible schools. Jane would have died of the malaria had it not been for a French nurse present at her bedside 24 hours a day for 3 days — night and day — giving her IV injections.

More than once, I had informed Jane and Joe's church about their preparation for the field, their language training and their needs during the time of sickness. Jane and Joe's picture adorned the large world map just outside the sanctuary. The statement: "Our Missionaries" graced the place next to their pictures. Jane and Joe received $120 a month before they actually got to Africa. After getting there, however, the support stopped.

As the church of 4,000 continued extolling the virtues of the bright new church carpet (paid for with cash), they prayed over it and blessed it to the tune of several thousands of dollars cash! Jane was wavering between life and death. My wife, Judy, wept uncontrollably because the church placed more value on their carpet than their malaria stricken missionaries in Africa whose pictures hung in

33

their foyer.

Luke 16 teaches us that money is a proving ground for discipleship. Giving is only a part of that discipleship. The book of Proverbs teaches that there are over fifteen categories of financial discipleship that we should consider. Other elements of financial discipleship thus either foster or hinder the missionary effort. Attitudes toward personal debt also play a role.

InterVarsity Christian fellowship hosts a large missions conference every few years called "Urbana." It attracts between 15,000 and 20,000 participants each time it is held on the University of Illinois campus in Urbana. The IVF speakers call for missions' commitments at the end of each of these conferences. Statistics show that only about 5% of those who respond actually make it to the mission field. The question we must ask and answer is "Why is this happening?"

Christianity Today magazine surveyed several hundred who had said "yes" at Urbana, but then did not go. They found disturbing information. *CT* found that a full 15% of these people who had made commitments at Urbana decided not to go to the mission field because of a student loan and the resulting financial strain it produced in their lives. Would it not be marvelous if the church of God decided to pay off these loans for the missionary at a pro-rata structured basis?-1 year in missions/year of school loan.

Awareness of the great expense involved in fulfilling the great commission is also strategic. Daniel (not his real name) is a Presbyterian missionary. God has used him in a powerful way in Korea. In fact, he is listed among the 100 most influential Christians in the history of the Korean church by a leading church historian in Korea. Daniel told me a remarkable money story.

One year he and his wife visited a large and prominent Presbyterian church in the USA. After preaching to the church, Daniel was told that the church had some good news for him and his family — they wanted to fully support them. They asked Daniel to send them a fully itemized budget of needs and expenses in detailed categories.

Daniel returned to Korea and dutifully filled out an itemized budget for the church as they had asked him to do. This itemized budget included schooling for his 3 children at the English speaking Seoul Foreign School to the tune of $5,000 per child/year. This detailed budget included the huge travel expenses for a ministry of his international stature and breadth. Indonesia and other third world nations cannot always finance guest speakers to come into their nations, so it falls upon people like Daniel to finance their own way, and it costs big money to go to these places. Many times Daniel has simply footed the bill as he went to the far interior of China, Nepal and other difficult spots. All these private expenses he and his family had borne for years without asking people for money — now he was finally able to tell a church the truth about his needs for his huge ministry efforts. All of this did not include the basic monthly living expenses of rent, lights, heat, clothing, health care and food.

Daniel submitted the budget to the church. The church was not pleased with what they read. Daniel's work was too expensive for them. They liked the Mercedes quality and reputation but wanted to pay a Kia price for it.

Jesus said that following Him would cost us our lives. For a church to follow Christ in giving will cost them big money. The price tag is high indeed.

Years back, one church asked its missionaries to submit an itemized budget. The missionaries again, dutifully, turned them in. The request was legitimate. One rather curious question graced the survey. The question asked the missionaries how much of their income they gave away. I know what two different responses from two different missionaries were. One missionary lied to the board not wanting them to know what he and his family had given away in the previous years. He was afraid that the church would have thought that they gave away too much and thus were bad stewards. The other missionary answered all of the questions on the survey except that same offensive last question. He wrote to the missions board the following note about that question: "I will be glad to tell you what I have given away last year under the following condition: Would each of you on the missions committee and each of the elders please write me and tell me what you gave away individually during the last year? If you tell me, I will be glad to tell you." Needless to say, the church did not ask this question again after that on their yearly review of the missionaries support.

Speaking of churches supporting missionaries, Pastor Oswald J. Smith of the People's Church in Toronto had these four cogent points about missionary support:

"1. If I refuse to give anything to missions this year, I practically cast a ballot in favor of the recall of every missionary.

2. If I give less than heretofore, I favor the reduction of the missionary forces proportionate to my reduced contribution.

3. If I give the same as formerly, I favor holding the ground already won; but I oppose any forward movement. My song is "Hold the Fort", forgetting that the Lord never intended His army to take refuge in a fort. All His soldiers are commanded to go.

4. If I increase my offering beyond the former years, then I favor an advance movement in the conquest of new territory for Christ."

(Oswald Smith, *The Challenge of Missions*, pg. 69, STL Books, UK.)

Responding to point 1: If the first century churches had understood Paul's dilemmas such as prison, hunger, thirst, cold, etc., the end of Philippians would be far different. Paul would have written that many churches had entered into the ministry of giving and receiving just like the Philippians. He pressed on through his own ingenuity to support himself and those with him.

Responding to point 2: I have more than one friend who has lost his missionary support because the home church went into debt for a new building project or some other debt.

Responding to point 3: Spiritual growth also covers growth in giving — giving in new areas and in new and larger dimensions.

Responding to point 4: How else will the church advance? We must have greater commitment from the missionaries on the field and great commitment from the saints at home supporting them.

In the midst of the difficult stories there are also good ones. One example of a giving church is in Minneapolis. God asked me to preach on the topic of giving to this fellowship. After the service, the pastor, Mark, took me to lunch. Over lunch, he and his wife, Karen, told me that they felt what I had said was truly from the Lord to them. They told me that God had challenged their church to give in the past in heightened ways.

Mark mentioned that they had invited one missionary with a large international ministry to speak at their church in 1989 for one Sunday morning and one Sunday evening service. They gave an honorarium to that missionary of $6,500. Another missionary with much work in Africa lead that same church in a 4-day missions conference as the main speaker. For this conference that church gave the missionary $15,000. This is unusual but beautiful! (Incidentally, the first missionary gave $5,500 to a Christian school of his choice. The second refused the honorarium, only to be told that the check had already been written and that it was a "done deal" as far as the church was concerned.) That missionary forwarded the check to needy Africa.

Ralph Winter wrote in *Perspectives on the World Christian Movement*,

"How hard have we tried to save others? The 2 billion dollars American evangelicals give to mission agencies is one-fourth of what they spend on weight-loss programs. A person must overeat by at least 2 dollars worth of food per month to maintain one excess pound of flesh. Yet 2 dollars per month is more than what 90% of all Christians in America give to missions. . . .

Winter continues,

"The essential tactic to adopt a wartime lifestyle is to build on pioneer mission perspective and to do so by a very simple and dramatic method. Those who are awakened from the grogginess and stupor of our times can, of course, go as missionaries. But, they can also stay home and deliberately and decisively adopt a missionary support level as their standard of living and their basis of lifestyle, regardless of their income. This will free up an unbelievable amount of money — so much, in fact, that if a million average Presbyterian households were to live within the average Presbyterian minister's salary, it would create at least two billion dollars a year. Yet, that happens to be only one-seventh of the amount Americans spend on tobacco." (p.706-707)

Ralph Winter's attitude is proper for equipping the warrior for battle. God wants well equipped and well provisioned soldiers in His army. Unfortunately, this is far from many church mentalities.

One church placed a rather severe constraint on its church members giving to a particular missionary couple working in northern India. This couple came from a South Pacific island without much opportunity of generating a homegrown support structure. They studied the language of Calcutta for a year and wanted to go back long-term for church planting and to reach an unreached people near the city.

A church in another Asian city took them on for support. The church decided to put a cap on the amount of support to give these two. The church told its members that every time they gave to that missionary and his wife (even privately), that they were to report it to the church missions board so that the missions board could deduct it from what they were giving the couple as a church promise. The reasons given by the head of the missions committee? - "We do not want to give them too much!" This is like the weapons supply officer saying to the people in the supply room, "Don't overload them with supplies. We don't want them to be too dangerous to the enemy!" Unfortunately, this story is played out thousands of times year after year in church after church around the world. Even if it is not verbalized in this way, the result is the same.

Charles Spurgeon said, "I have heard of the stewardess on an American vessel, who, when the ship was sinking, saw heaps of gold coin scattered upon the cabin floor by those who had thrown it there in the confusion of their escape. She gathered up large quantities of it, wrapped it around her waist and leaped into the water. She sank like a millstone, as though she had studiously prepared herself for destruction." Unfortunately, our attitudes reflect that stewardess at times when it comes to missions giving.

In Scripture, we see two pictures of God's level of generosity, one in the Old Testament, one in the New Testament. In 1 Chronicles 29:1-4, King David leaves his reign to Solomon. He introduces Solomon.

King David financed and led in the support raising for building the temple of God under Solomon.

David describes his personal offering in terms of

gold, silver, metals and precious stones. David told all of the people that he gave 3,000 talents of gold to the work of building the temple of God. One talent weighs 75.8 pounds or about 35 kilograms. This comes to a contemporary figure of about $1.8 billion — a remarkable amount of money for one man to give in one offering on one day.

Let us suppose that David put his money in an investment that makes interest at 10% a year. This means that David would be getting at least $160 million US Dollars per year on that money without touching the principal.

With the interest alone, David could have purchased 2,000 Mercedes Benz autos at $75,000 per car. He could have purchased 55,000 Rolex watches at $3,000 per watch. He could have done this on and on into eternity without ever even touching the principal of that 1.6 billion dollars. David chose rather to donate it to the work of God.

Suppose David were alive today. David could support 6,000 missionaries at the figure stated by the US Center for World Missions of $26,000 per year. David could have supported them eternally with just the interest off his principal. This is truly God's level of giving.

If you are like me, you find it difficult to relate to David's giving due to his wealth. The New Testament relates the story of a poor widow who gave everything she had in Mark 12. We can all relate to this widow's lack of wealth, though probably not to her level of giving.

Charles Colson stated, "Only 25% of evangelicals tithe. While 40% say faith in God is the most important thing in their lives. Those who make between $50,000 and $75,000 per year give only an average of 1.5% to charity, religious or otherwise. This same group spends 12% of their income on leisure pursuits." (*The Body*, Charles Colson, p.31)

To help our missionaries, we must do better than this. Larry and Becky are former missionaries. They ministered on several continents for several years on a shoestring. As they worked for the Lord, God gave them two kids and because they could not get above a shoestring existence, they are now home. Larry worked in an old folks home and then went back into a pastorate. They simply got tired of fighting it for money. This story is heard over and over in missions.

There are still the bright spots. In the mid-1970's, Pastor Cho was in the process of building his famous church on Yoido Island in Seoul, Korea. This church is now the largest one (in number of members) in the 2000 years history of God's church worldwide.

As they were building a $5 million US Dollar sanctuary, only the walls and floor were finished. Pastor Cho desired to build his church with Korean money. Every night for three months he would get out of bed and cross the bedroom floor to the opposite corner to cry. His wife thought he was going crazy.

As the deadline for the $5 million payment drew near, the church held special all night prayer meetings. At one of these meetings, Pastor Cho spoke about the need for money to build the church and faith. At the end of the message, Cho experienced the preacher's nightmare: Having called for giving commitments to the church building project signified by a trip to the altar, nobody moved. Silence haunted the sanctuary. As the uncomfortable silence continued, finally, it was broken by an unlikely candidate.

An old grandmother slowly rose from her pew and moved to the front of the partially built church. (It was winter and was freezing with no windows, doors or roof.) She hobbled to the front with her cane. Arriving at the altar, every eye was riveted on her. She placed a rice bowl, two chopsticks and a spoon on the altar. Pastor Cho began to cry and lifted these items from the altar to give back to the lady. The grandmother replied, "Pastor, would not God receive what an old dying lady has to give Him to build His church?" So, he took back the rice bowl, two chopsticks and spoon and replaced them on the altar. She turned and began hobbling back to her pew.

A businessman shouted from the back of the incomplete sanctuary, "Pastor, I will buy that rice bowl, those two chopsticks and that spoon for the equivalent of $30,000 US Dollars." God opened heaven that night and the church was financed with Korean money. How did it start? A rice bowl, two chopsticks and a spoon.

I believe God wants to challenge us with a rice bowl, two chopsticks and a spoon. How much are they worth to us?

Connecting missionary money to missionary problems is an easy task. So, our thinking flows naturally to consider missionary personal problems in the following chapter.

Phil Parshall asked 390 missionaries from all parts of the world,

"What is your greatest spiritual struggle in life?"

The three highest percentage responses were...
- Maintaining a successful devotional life
- Having spiritual victory
- Lust

—Phil Parshall
How Spiritual Are Missionaries?

CHAPTER THREE

Personal Problems Among Missionaries
or Are You There, God? It's Me, Your Missionary

What a wretched man I am! Who will rescue me from this body of death?"

—*Romans 7:24*

IT'S PROBABLY NOT hard for you to picture the idyllic life of a missionary. Let's see: Sleeping late, fishing with the 'natives,' living in a hut, no stresses of the 'real' world.

Right.

Out on the field, things are a little different. In fact, it might not even be a 'field' at all. Missionaries are planted all over the world, including the middle of large urban areas. Yes, it is true that, as a missionary, some of the challenges of home are no longer relevant. But, replace them with anxiety, fear, burnout, culture shock, inability to adjust, being confronted with questions that have no answer, lust, emotional problems and a lack of ability to maintain a consistent devotional life, and it's a whole new ballgame.

Phil Parshall, who once surveyed 390 missionaries from all over the world, found that more than 20% had taken tranquilizers while on the mission field. And, more than 70% of those surveyed described anger as either a significant or frequent part of their lives (from *Helping Missionaries Grow* by Kelly and Michele O'Donnell). So, what's going on here? To give you an idea, I'll start with a few stories of my own.

In 1991, my wife Judy and I went to Uganda and Kenya. We started by getting our visas for Kenya while still in the United States; we also received our visas for Uganda. On the way to Uganda, however, while staying overnight in Kenya, the Kenyan authorities canceled our visas. That meant that two weeks later, when we came back to Kenya to preach, they made us buy two more visas, at the hefty price of $80 each. It was pure manipulation; while we were still in the United States, we had called the Kenyan consulate to make sure that this was exactly what we didn't need to do. To say that we were angry would be accurate; but we had no choice. We paid our $160 and went on.

Of course, missionary difficulties reach back as far as the Bible. Paul himself, in 2 Corinthians 11, discussed some of the dangers of the ministry. In 2 Corinthians 11:28, he mentions anxiety. Remember, this is the same apostle who taught the Philippians to be anxious for nothing. Aren't the realism and honesty of the Scriptures beautiful? There is indeed room for both paradox and contradiction in life; it may not be logical, but at least we know it's Biblical!

Anyway, back to Kenya. While there, I experienced fear — real fear — for one of the first times in my missionary life. Our work in Kenya was in an area of East Africa widely known for its theft problem. One outreach team from Europe found out the hard way: they were completely stripped of their clothing. After being surrounded and accosted by a truckload of Kenyan thieves, they were forced to walk back to the missionary compound in their underwear. Every single one of the students there had been robbed on the street at one time or another.

Our missionary bungalow, I should mention, was surrounded by a high fence with bars on all the windows. The atmosphere was made complete with guard dogs — ferocious guard dogs — as well as a night watchman with a stick that looked like a glorified baseball bat. (Though he was well armed, this watchman was not nearly so well prepared as his counterpart in Uganda, who sported an AK-47 sub-machine gun in the Anglican compound. Needless to say, we weren't as scared in Uganda!)

The night before leaving the eastern part of Kenya for Nairobi, I was told by a missionary in Likoni that the thieves in Nairobi were different from those in Likoni. Although Likoni is known for its theft, the missionary explained, thieves there don't normally kill their victims. Yet, he said, in Nairobi the thieves kill their victims just because they want to. After that, I wasn't exactly looking forward to my two-night stay in Nairobi. Because I had so much fear in my heart, I literally slept less than four hours during my entire time there.

Apparently things haven't changed that much for missionaries through the years: Paul, too, wrote that he was in danger from robbers. As for my wife, she had a close encounter while in Hong Kong a few years back. She strolled into her room on the missionary base just in time to find a woman rifling through her belongings in search of money. Earlier that day, Judy had cashed checks for several other missionaries, totaling thousands of dollars. Thankfully, the Lord stepped in before everyone lost a lot of money!

Aside from robbery, however there's a much more insidious attack against missionaries: the feeling that they've got to the take 'the world for Christ.'

Too often, that leads directly to burnout.

According to psychologists, those in 'people helping' professions are most susceptible to burnout. And missionaries, of course, would be at the top of that list.

More than one friend has suffered — or still suffers — from chronic fatigue syndrome. A few of my missionary friends have had to leave the field and check into a hospital due to burnout and overwork.

Remember Parshall and his study of missionaries? In it, he found that stress and tension were significant problems in the lives of more than 70% of those surveyed. It's no wonder that so many had used tranquilizers like Valium. One friend publicly testified that she was so burned out that more than once she had folded herself up into a fetal position in the bottom of her closet, just wanting the world to go away. And this is one who had ministered on every continent, in more than 50 countries. The problems and the pain are all too real.

It would seem that the answers to these and other emotional struggles would be readily available through prayer, Bible study, meditation, and the like. But, according to a 1983 study by Raymond Chester, a shocking 68% of the missionaries surveyed didn't seek spiritual solutions to their stress problems. It's no wonder, then, that when Parshall did his study four years later, he found that maintaining a devotional life was consistently the biggest problem stated by an overwhelming majority of those on the mission field. In addition, anger proved to be a problem for 88% of the missionaries who responded, and 17% stated that they frequently struggled with it. Lust ranked highly on the list of spiritual problems, too, with a surprising 70% describing it as a struggle and 18% battling it frequently. Some 70% of the missionaries experienced discouragement, and 31% were often emotionally tense.

Idyllic, right? During the Third Annual Conference on Mental Health and Missions, Stanley and Brent Lindquist shared some case histories. One man in the middle of his first term overseas, they said, had severe problems with cultural adjustment and attempted suicide. He had to be resuscitated. (It should be noted that, after some time of therapy, he returned to the field, and was, at last report, functioning well.)

As for another woman who had been a missionary for fourteen years, she began having sexual delusions on the field and was forced to return home. It took therapy and a time of rest to return to normal, but she eventually went on to an on-going successful career. In a third case, an 18-year veteran was admitted to intensive psychotherapy for severe depression. After a few months, he overdosed on his medication, necessitating heroic measure for saving his life. Unfortunately, his family left the field permanently; but they are pursuing successful careers at home.

And then there's the other emotional attack: the draw of sexual sin.

George Verwer, founder of Operation Mobilization, considers it a result of missionary burnout. But, what are the warning signs? What steps can be taken to keep this from happening? We can start by recognizing the warning signs of burnout itself: constant depression, loss of missionary vision, irritability, tiredness, disorientation and the like. To start, missionaries should be active participants in a regular accountability group. (By regular, I mean weekly, biweekly or monthly.)

Ruth Tucker, author of *Guardians of the Great Commission,* wrote much about the personal problems of missionaries. In addition to sin, there was sacrifice. Here's an account of missionary legend David Livingstone:

"By 1852, after seven years of marriage, Livingstone was no longer able to defend the severe health risks to which his exploratory work exposed his family. Yet, he chose not to settle down, but to send his family back to England and continue his exploration alone. "Nothing but a strong conviction that the step will tend to the glory of Christ," he wrote, "would make me orphanize my children." His exploration did have a powerful impact on missionary work in Africa, but he paid a heavy price for it — a price for which he himself showed remorse. To his wife, he wrote:

"My dearest Mary — how I miss you now, and the dear children. My heart yearns incessantly over you. How many thoughts of the past crowd into my mind. I feel as if I would treat you all the more tenderly and lovingly than ever…I never show my feelings; but I can say truly, my dearest, that I loved you when I married you, and the longer I lived with you, I loved you the better."

For Mary, it was a painful separation, and adjusting to life back in England was most difficult. She and the children had a miserable existence. They were "homeless and friendless" and "often on the edge of poverty in cheap lodging." Mary Livingstone was said to be drowning her sorrows in alcohol." (Ibid p.19)

So, was Livingstone right in doing what he did — scripturally right? Different people would say different things.

But, Livingstone was not alone in his agony; that's for sure. Ruth Tucker goes on:

The pain of watching a child die an agonizing death was only matched by the suffering caused by the death of a newborn baby — a scenario which was all too common for missionary mothers. Mary Williams, who would later lose her husband to the cannibals of the South Sea Islands, is an example. In 1831, she was pregnant again and "hoped by a change of scene, that she might be spared the distress of consigning a seventh sweet babe to a premature grave." But, once again misfortune struck and "yet another still-born infant was 'planted' in the soil of yet another tropical island. The pain was nearly unbearable, but Mary had no choice but to pick up the pieces and go on with life."

Hudson Taylor and his wife, Maria, also faced premature death of their children. The oldest of their five kids, Gracie, died of water on the brain at 8 years old. Maria's sixth child, a boy named Sammy, died at five years old. Maria was pregnant at the time of Sammy's death, and the baby she bore not long after lived less than two weeks. Maria herself died just three days later.

Jonathan and Rosalind Goforth, missionary legends to China, lost five of their 11 children in infancy or childhood. Let's consider the apostles of the first century here, too. Most of them were martyred. Talk about stress!

In 1983, Dorothy Gish wrote about the sources of missionary stress in the *Journal of Psychology and Theology*. As part of the article, Gish included a table of sources of stress identified by at least 30% of the respondents. For her study, 556 missionaries from several different countries in Africa and Australia were surveyed.

The first percentage figure listed represents 'much stress;' the second, 'great stress.'

Have a look:

Much Stress   Great Stress

Confronting others when necessary
54   27

Communicating across language cultural barrier
53   26

Time and effort maintaining donor relationships
50   22

Amount of work
48   25

Work priorities
47   18

Time for personal study of the Word and prayer
37   14

Progress on my work
36   14

Need for pastoral care
35   15

Making decisions affecting others' lives
35   15

Need acceptance including self-forgiveness
34   4

Conflicts between my values and host culture's
34   13

Goldfish bowl experience
33   13

Certainty about my future
33   13

Freedom to take time for myself
32   12

Extended family concerns	
31	12
Frequent moving	
31	18
Task orientation vs. servant attitude	
31	11
Recreation and exercise	
30	9

In one study among Conservative Baptist missionaries, it was discovered that 50% of those who left the field early did so because of a physical or emotional health problem. This is significant. In one study, 10% of denominational missionaries had long-term debilitating illnesses, predominantly fatigue and glandular dysfunction, which continued on for years with little improvement. Many have remained on the field working only at half productivity or less. One study suggests that missionaries don't realize how stressed out they really are. (Some credit for psychological/sociological research in this chapter must go to Kelly and Michele O'Donnell who wrote *Helping Missionaries Grow.* The O'Donnell's have also written two other books on the same topic: *Missionary Care:Counting the Cost for World Evangelization* and also *Doing Member Care Well, Perspectives and Practices from Around the World.* Some of the research in this chapter is original with me, the only problem is that I don't know which is original with them and which parts I actually went to the original sources on. The facts are correct though.)

Some missionaries may not be realizing, either, just how much culture shock is affecting them. Wayne Dye, in a report to the American Society of Missiology, admitted that he didn't expect to still be experiencing culture shock after several years of living among the Bahinemo.

"But I was," he said. "Furthermore, I was not alone. In anthropology seminars, it became apparent that quite a number of field workers continue to experience stress after many years of living in a village. From reading the literature, we consultants had expected that the shock would be over in a couple of years; the very term "shock" implies something that is severe but brief.

Culture shock is caused by the "anxiety that results from losing all our familiar signs and symbols of social intercourse." he went on. "These field workers, however, already knew a variety of cultural cures and used them in communication with the villagers. Yet they were still under strain. Even field workers with considerable education and preparation experienced these problems."

One linguist, Dye reported, found himself kicking toads on the path.

Apparently, it's not just the adults who are affected, either. A 1983 study of missionary kids studying at boarding schools in America showed that their three most common difficulties were (a.) longing for foreign lands; (b.) culture shock; and (c.) no sense of loyalty or commitment to a local church.

As for the last one, it's closely related to relational ties as a whole. Wondering how bad these can get? The Lindquists, who presented their case studies before the Third Annual Conference on Mental Health and Missions, detailed one situation in which a couple had originally been described as "well adjusted with very few difficulties." (*ibid*, O'Donnell"

As the interview continued, the Lindquists found that the missionaries had actually been "very frustrated with the national people, feeling that they were all liars, that the only reason they were interested in talking to Americans was to get visas to get out of the country, and that they would just as soon stab you in the back." With that kind of relationship to the nationals, "well adjusted" no longer applies. (*ibid*, O'Donnell"

Yet, as we look back to Paul, we find that relationship hassles were a problem in his ministry, too. In Acts, remember, we read about Paul and Barnabas arguing over whether young Mark should continue on with them in the ministry. Thankfully, that relationship break was eventually healed.

In dealing with relationships with the "natives." however, missionaries encounter all sorts of situations that they probably never could have dreamed of.

We can start with bizarre religious doctrines.

Jackie Pullinger, missionary to the outcasts on the streets of Hong Kong, told of a recent heresy that was most popular in southern mainland China.

It all started when a pastor walked to a village in China, not far from his own. He was on his way to preach a Sunday morning service, but along the way, he became thirsty and decided to stop at an open-faced well for a drink of water. As the story goes, the pastor leaned over the well, but lost his balance. He fell head over heels, right into the well. Fortunately, his foot caught on the well rope, and he became entangled. He ended up being suspended, upside down in the well, for about 45 minutes. After a time of calling for help, some of the villagers came and rescued him from the well, and he went on to the church and preached.

After the service, members of the church commented that his preaching was the most moving and powerful they had ever heard coming from him. They asked him what he had done differently this time to prepare, and as he considered his response, only one thing came to mind: the time he had spent in the well. Because he had spent that time suspended, he reasoned, God had anointed him in a special way.

You can probably guess what came next. All

through one of the provinces in southern China, preachers began regularly suspending themselves upside down over open-faced wells before church.

Ultimately, someone had to correct this kind of teaching.

That's not the only bizarre story from China, either. Another Hong Kong missionary told of a man who sacrificed his son, thinking that God was requiring of him what He required of Abraham with Isaac.

All over the world, however, missionaries are called upon to make calls on what is right. Yes, they have the Scriptures as a guide. But, even with the word of God, things are not always clear. When I teach my Bible classes, I confront the young missionary students with a tough little quiz early on in the year. Basically, it comes down to this: Which things must be corrected, and which can simply be left alone? To illustrate the point, we look at Bible passages and consider whether they apply in all situations.

Why not see how well you do with this little quiz yourself?

Temporary or Permanent?

Taken from *The Christian Leader*, Nov. 9, 1976

A major problem for any missionary who is trying to communicate cross-culturally is the need to separate gospel from that which is merely cultural or temporary. People should not have to become Americans/Westerners — or first century Greeks — in order to become Christians.

As it turns out, the job of separating that which is permanent from that which is temporary is important not only for cross-cultural missionaries, but for all Christians as well. Which of the specific practices and commands that appear in the New Testament are to apply at all times in all places? Which are merely temporary, needed at one particular time in one particular place, but not necessarily applicable at other times and in other places?

If you'd like to get a handle on the problem, we suggest you try this self-think exercise adapted from material put together by a former missionary in Ethiopia. We've listed 50 practices and commands that appear in the New Testament. In that sense, all are "Scriptural." The question is, which are meant to be permanent (P) and which merely temporary (T)?

Think about each one, then mark each one with a P or T. Of course, there will be some you're not too sure about (welcome to the mission field!)

____ "Greet one another with a holy kiss" (Rom 16:16).

____ Abstain from meat that has been sacrificed to idols (Acts 15:29).

____ Be baptized (Acts 2:38).

____ "A woman ought to have a veil on her head" (I Cor 11:10).

____ Wash each other's feet (John 13:14.

____ Extend the "right hand (Left hand?) of fellowship" (Gal 2:9).

____ Ordain by the "laying on of hands" (Acts 13:3).

____ "It is indecent for a woman to speak in an assembly" (I Cor 14:35).

____ Have fixed hours of prayer (Acts 3:1).

____ Sing "songs, hymns, and spiritual songs" (Col 3:16).

____ Abstain from eating blood (Acts 15:29).

____ Observe "festivals, new moons, and Sabbaths" (Col. 2:16).

____ Observe the Lord's Supper (I Cor. 11:24).

____ "Remember the poor" (Gal 3:10).

____ Anoint the sick with oil (James).

____ "Permit no woman to teach men" (I Tim 2:12).

____ Preach two by two (Mark 6:7).

____ Speak Greek in the assembly (Acts 14:1).

____ "Eat what is set before you asking no questions" (I Cor 10:27).

____ Prohibit women from wearing braided hair, gold or pearls (I Tim 2:12).

____ Abstain from fornication (Acts 15:29).

____ "Do not seek marriage" (I Cor 7:27).

____ Be circumcised (Acts 15:5).

____ Refuse to eat reptiles or "birds of the air" (Acts 10:12).

____ Drink communion from a single cup (Mark 14:24).

____ Take formal religious vows (Acts 1818).

____ Refrain from public prayer (Mt. 6:5,6).

____ Speak in tongues (I Cor 14:5).

____ Meet in homes for church (Co. 4:15).

____ "Work with your hands" (I Thess 4:11)

____ Lift your hands when praying (I Tim 2:8).

____ "Give to those who beg from you" (Mt 5:42).

____ Pray before meals (Lk 24:30)

____ "Enroll no widow under 60 years old" (I Tim 5:9).

____ Say "Amen" at the end of prayers (I Cor 14:16).

____ Fast in connection with ordination (Acts 13:3).

____ "Beware of Dogs" (Phil 3:2).

____ "Wives be subject to your husbands" (Col 3:18).

____ "Show no partiality" toward the rich (James 2:1-7).

____ Use unleavened bread for communion (Lk 22:13,19).

____ Cast lots for church officers (Acts 1:26).

____ "Owe no man anything" (Rom 13:8).

_____ Have seven deacons in the church (Acts 6).

_____ Abstain from meat of animals killed by strangulation (Acts 15:29).

_____ "If anyone will not work, let them not eat" (2 Thess 3:10).

_____ Worship on Saturday (Acts 13:14, 42,44).

_____ Sell lands and house when one becomes a Christian (Acts 4:32-37).

_____ Have self-employed clergy (I Thess 3:7-8).

_____ Take collections in church for the poor (I Cor 16:1).

_____ Refuse to take oaths (Mt 6:33-37).

Now that you're finished, get ready for the hard part. Ask yourself what principle you used to distinguish the ones that are permanent and essential from those that are merely temporary and cultural. Since you made a separation, you must have used some standard. But what was it? Remember: Your principle must be one that can apply to every example in the above list.

Write out that principle. You might try saying something like, "All commands or practices which...are permanent, and all those which...are temporary." Then, just to keep yourself honest, have a friend examine your categories for a second opinion on how well you held to your example.

How'd you do? There really is no answer key in the text, and therein lies the problem. Sometimes it really is difficult to apply the Bible correctly. And that's just as true in cross-cultural situations as anywhere else.

Consider, for example, the idea of a "foot-washing service." In America, it's quite acceptable. Yet, in Thailand, such a service would be culturally offensive and inappropriate.

In parts of Europe, greeting each other with a holy kiss is acceptable. But, it's quite unacceptable in parts of Asia. In the West, abstaining from meat offered to idols is not a significant issue. Yet, if you travel to Singapore, Hong Kong or Taiwan, and ask the Christians there if this is controversial, they'll decidedly say yes.

Though these issues may seem problematic, they seem almost simple compared to the experiences of some. For instance, consider the following two scenarios, both of them very real.

Let's start with the Duvle people, a small group of about 205 hunter-gatherers living in the lakes area of Irian Jaya, Indonesia. They live in two villages of about 100 each, and they eat wild pigs and fish.

In the early 1960's, a nearby tribe called the Dani was evangelized. Alexander Bolyanatz, a Wycliffe missionary consultant and anthropology Professor, stated that "significant portions" converted to

Christianity. Traditionally the Danis and the Duvles were enemies, but in 1964, representatives of the Duvles went to a missionary outpost to find out if the Danis truly wanted to stop fighting.

Local Danis assured the Duvles that this was the case. Then, the Duvles asked for a Christian representative to come to their villages and tell them the same message that the Danis had been told.

A year later, Dani evangelists had settled in a Duvle village, and the village grew greatly as a result of the evangelists' arrival. Dr. Bolyanatz puts the growth rate at 50%. And, within 20 years, over half of the adult Duvle tribe had converted.

Doesn't sound like a problem, does it? Consider, however, that the Danis brought more than the gospel with them; they also brought their own culture. Dani music, for example, was introduced as the "Christian worship" music style. In addition, the Duvle men began cutting their usually long hair in direct response to the Dani style — which once was also long but now is short — because of the missionaries. This was probably due to the idea that shorter hair was more hygienic, Bolyanatz stated. And speaking of hygiene, the Duvles began bathing due to Dani influence, too. Formerly, bathing was only considered important for younger children.

It sounds as though everything went over without a hitch, though that wasn't quite the case. One change the Dani wanted to bring about met with resistance.

The Dani tribesmen wore gourds over their penises for protection. The Duvles, on the other hand, wore barkcloth aprons as traditional garb. For the Dani evangelists, these barkcloth aprons were much too unrefined for anyone "aspiring to be a Christian." But, the barkcloth aprons have stayed. In fact, Bolyanatz stated, "penis gourds have been attached to children as a joke — a not too clearly camouflaged epithet aimed at the Dani."

As for the women, Bolyanatz mentioned that they were asked to change their bark skirts to grass skirts, but refused. In his footnotes, however, Bolyanatz wrote that the Duvle soon began to wear more "normal" Indonesian clothing, encouraged by the government of Indonesia.

"Women enjoy sarongs or small striped sheets as wrap-around skirts for minimum clothing and T-shirts for special occasions. Men prefer drawstring swim trunks and tank tops for everyday use and knee-length pants and T-shirts as formal attire."

In addition, Bolyanatz stated that, "Dani men, especially those with a position such as pastor or evangelist, now wear at least knee-length pants and T-shirts. Most Dani women still wear grass or string skirts, with T-shirts as well." (quoted and cited by permission from "Differentiated Responses to Evangelization: A Case Study from Irian Jaya." Paper presented to the American Anthropological Assn. Session on "Christianity and Colonialism", November, 1989, Alexander Bolyanatz, Ph.D.)

Now, when it comes to being an evangelist, where do you draw the line with something as culturally basic as clothing? One Mennonite missionary, home from a tropical area, was asked if she had taught the natives to be "simple in dress." The missionary replied, "We are lucky to get them to wear clothes." How does the missionary relate this to a conservative North American congregation in a newsletter? As for our second scenario, it comes from a people called the Kaka, in Eastern Cameroon, Africa.

The Kaka structure is Biblically confused, to say the least, and the idea of introducing Christian ethics into such a structure is more than a challenge. For example, a Kaka man considers many to be his "wife." They include (a.) any wives of a maternal uncle; (b.) the wives of his older brother; and (c.) his wife's younger sisters. A Kaka man may not have sex with the wife of his older brother, but he may have sex with his wife's younger sister. After the younger sisters get married, however, "this is less frequent." The response of the Kaka man is, "For this reason it is advisable to marry an older sister always so that you can get the younger one, too, later on."

Whew. As for premarital sex, a young girl is, "free to indulge in sexual promiscuity as often and with as many males as she chooses." As a result, (wrote missionary William Reyburn in his paper titled *Kaka Kinship, Sex, and Adultery* in 1958), "a girl picks up dozens of suitors. These males never relinquish their claims on the girl even after marriage. Consequently, her premarital suitors often continue to seek relations after marriage."

The question we must answer is, does the gospel make a difference in this culture? Reyburn responds: "Sexual perversions, prostitution, and other institutions are making themselves felt right along with the endeavors to maintain standards of Christian tradition. In this conflicting picture of multiple stresses, the Kaka are sure only with the familiar direction of the residence group in clan. Consequently, a Christianity which does not make itself intelligible on familiar grounds runs the chance of becoming irrelevant."

Further, let's take a closer look at the African concept of productivity. Africans are oriented toward productivity on the basis of what constitutes the "good life." As long as productivity leads to the "good," then all things associated with productivity are "good." That's how a Kaka philosopher might put it, anyway. And to continue, premarital relations, extramarital relations, extreme sexual plurality of wives, and many children are all aspects of the "good life." The Christian doesn't entirely give up this African view of the "good." However, as a Christian, he is expected to transform the value and association of productivity. And that transformation doesn't come automatically when he becomes a church member.

Walter Trobisch, a pioneer with Inter-Varsity, discusses similar problems among youth in Cameroon when it comes to sex and marriage. He surveyed 22 unmarried male students who had attended a Christian mission school for 11 years. Apparently, all the lessons didn't sink in. He writes in his article "*Pre-Marital Relations and Christian Marriage in Africa*, 1961:"

"In general, these boys think today that premarital sexual relations are not only useful, but indispensable. There are believed to be greater advantages gained through premarital relations than bad consequences to be suffered. The reasons they gave can be divided into two groups, physical and psychological.

Physical reasons given include the following:

The sexual desire "never leaves one." The sex organs must be exercised in order to avoid underdevelopment and atrophy. "Because these organs exist, they have to function."

The girl should be tested for suitability before marriage for a variety of strange reasons.

Psychological reasons included the theory of learning by doing. "Before you go hunting, you have to sharpen your spear" (an African proverb). Some of these boys claimed that the instruction in natural sciences and experiments in physics and chemistry have strengthened this argument and have awakened the "taste for experimenting." A major motive was to avoid being mocked by other boys and also girls. "What do you think you are? Do you want to be holier than all of us? You are just a coward."

Trobisch further writes that, "If a girl would suggest to a boy that he may be impotent, the boy has virtually no other way of proving to her contrary than having sexual intercourse with her."

The problems don't stop there. Eskimo husbands, for example, are very "open" when it comes to hospitality. In order to show the hospitality to traveling friends, they share their wives for a night or two as the friends pass through. The favor, of course, is reciprocated when friends have shown hospitality to other friends, and later travel. Eugene Nida, a missionary researcher, mentioned that there is no apparent jealousy or distrust among the Eskimos engendered by this practice. Even so, it is up to the missionaries to address the problem from the point of view of the Scriptures — and hopefully, to bring about a change in the Eskimo culture. Changes like that don't come easy, however.

Take a look at another example from northern African Congo. Nida describes the scene for us: "But we are not going to have our wives dress like prostitutes," protested an elder in the Ngbaka church in northern Congo, as he replied to the suggestion made by the missionary that the women should be required to wear blouses to cover their breasts. The church leaders were unanimous in objecting to such a requirement, for in that part of Congo, the well-dressed and fully dressed African women were too often prostitutes, since they alone had the money to spend on attractive garments. Different peoples are in wide disagreement as to the amount or type of clothes required by modesty. Not long ago, one of the chiefs in the Micronesian island of Yap forbade any woman coming into the town with a blouse. However, he insisted that all women would have to wear grass skirts reaching almost to the ankles. To the Yapese way of thinking, bare legs are a sign of immodesty, while the uncovered breasts are perfectly proper. (p. 1, *Customs and Cultures,* Nida.)

Again, we can look back to the Bible and know that there is nothing new under the sun. Paul had to solve problems of prostitution, ungodly sexual ethics and basic immorality with the people in Corinth.

It's true, then, that the problems that plague the missionaries of today — emotional problems, relational issues, adjustment difficulties, culture shock, raw stress and human need — are universal.

Not too long ago, I was asked to speak as a part of a missions conference for a Baptist church. They told me, interestingly enough, that it wasn't necessary for me to talk about money. So, I decided to talk about the other harsh realities of the mission field.

It should be noted here that the church supports some 26 missionaries. And the night before my turn to speak, the missions committee held a forum. One by one, 10 long-term missionaries detailed their struggles before their supporting congregation.

Many broke down and publicly wept onstage because of the pain in their lives.

Needless to say, it was the perfect introduction to my message the following night. I talked about the realities of the mission field as I saw them, and afterward, one of the elder missionaries who had worked in Africa for more than 20 years leaned over to the head of the mission board and said, "Praise God! It's about time somebody said this!"

It bears repeating, too.

An idyllic life? No.

But, an important one? Yes.

CHAPTER FOUR

Missionary Failures

A HIGH-POWERED rocket slammed into the fuselage of Korean airliner 007. The world mourned corporately as we watched the news programs detail the savage attack. There were Christians on that airliner.

Only a few days earlier, Princess Diana's birthday party occurred. She had invited a beautiful young Korean friend to her party. After Princess Di's friend arrived in England, she received a long distance phone call from Korea. The young Korean's mother told her daughter to come home immediately because she felt an urgency from God to do so. Not wanting to displease her mother, she re-booked her flight back to Seoul, leaving London ahead of time. Two cabin attendants on the KAL flight invited her to move up to first class so that they could talk and find out more about her since she was so beautiful. She took her Bible along and eventually led those two attendants to the Lord right there on the plane.

The beautiful young Korean arrived home not knowing why God, through her mother, was so insistent on her early return.

The following few days tragically played themselves out as the original flight on which that young woman was to be flying home was shot out of the sky. Two new Christians were on the plane — the flight attendants.

Evangelism teams went through outlying villages in Korea shortly after this tragedy. Unfortunately, immature Christians made up large percentages of those teams and were "evangelizing" a hurting nation with "good news" from Christ. Sadly, the "gospel" they preached was not presented properly. These well meaning people were commanding the Korean listeners to first forgive the Russians for shooting down their airliner before they accepted Christ. Needless to say, this only led to scorn in the villages and a total false perception of what the gospel was.

Missionary failure comes in various forms. This one is an example of preaching a gospel that is harsher than the demands of God. God demands repentance and faith in Christ for salvation. The Bible declares nothing about national forgiveness as a condition of salvation. This type of false teaching does not necessarily originate with immature believers on foreign soil. From American pulpits millions are influenced every week by a gospel that is not always Biblical. Paul wrote Timothy to "entrust to faithful men" what Paul had earlier taught Timothy. This is more important than ever in the "missions sending" national churches.

George Barna wrote about the values and religious views of Americans in *What Americans Believe.* His method was to survey people across the United States by asking: "You have a responsibility to explain your religious beliefs to others who may believe differently." "Do you agree strongly, agree somewhat, disagree somewhat, or disagree strongly with that statement?" His findings were troubling — only 28% strongly believe that they have a responsibility to share their Christian beliefs with others who have a different set of beliefs. An equivalent proportion "feel strongly that they do not have any such obligation." (*What Americans Believe,* George Barna, p.220) In many respects, missionary failure is being set up in the pulpits of "evangelized nations." Barna found that only 43% of the population who claim to be born again believe that they are responsible to evangelize lost people. The failure begins at home.

Eugene Nida wrote in *Customs and Cultures,* "...where missionary work has been singularly unsuccessful, one will always find a failure to resolve the missionary's two great problems: identification (with the culture) and communication (language issues.)" (p.251) He goes further to describe how "A Pagan looks at Missionary Work." I quote Nida, the Wycliffe missionary statesman, at length on this.

> To the average "pagan" the Christian message is both puzzling and disconcerting. The insistence upon uniting religion and morality often seems weird. How can spirits, who are themselves unpredictably mischievous, be concerned with ethical behavior? To the Quecha Indian who declared, "Our gods are all drunkards and so are we," the missionary's talk about sobriety as a part of religion seems foolishness.
>
> Furthermore, most people argue, "Religion is a specialty — a job for priests, shamen, sorcerers and seers. It is not for me, and certainly can have no claim upon all of life." Many Navajos abhor the idea of worshiping a dead man who rose again and who offers to live in their hearts by means of His Spirit (i.e. his ghost — as they understand it). Their almost pathological fear of the spirits of the dead makes the preaching of the resurrection more than simply "a stumbling block" or "foolishness." In the eyes of many Africans the God of Christianity is either cheap or stupid, for he requires no continual sacrifices. How can one establish an advantage in bargaining without putting God under obligation by the requisite offerings of

meal and blood and the careful recital of secret words? A missionary's denunciations against smoking tobacco seem almost blasphemous to the man who thinks that the acrid smell of dense tobacco smoke induces more perfect communion with his god.

Nevertheless, it is not primarily the message by the messenger of the Christianity that provides the greater problems for the average non-Christian. Fortunately, the missionary who shouts at "natives" as he would at a dog and who by threatening corporal punishment forces the people to build chapels and to till the soil is the exception to the rule; but those well-intentioned victims of a superiority complex who exude a holier-than-thou condescension full of paternalistic piety still delude themselves into thinking that their task is to work for people rather than with them. Their unsuspected self-righteousness and their identification of western culture with Christianity keeps them from spiritual comradeship. They remain foreign, not only in the outward phases of race and culture, but also in the inward emotional responses. Gross insensitiveness in one mission resulted in a program for the training of "native leadership" which requires the young preachers to be separated from their families for almost eleven out of twelve months over a period of nearly eight years, during which time they are to prove their spirituality by abject submission to authority as evidenced in their doing drudge work.

A missionary's failure to identify himself with the people, not in sympathy but in empathy, is sometimes made more acute by reluctance, inability, or callousness to the proper use of the people's language. Communication is essentially a two-way experience; one must understand before he can talk, one must learn before he can also help to open the culture — closed heart of a missionary to the unsuspected needs and aspirations of the people."

(Used by permission, *Customs and Cutures*, p.251, 252)

Paul preached on Mars Hill in Athens. He used terms, metaphors, stories and traditions that the Athenians could relate to. The responsibility for us to do the same thing has not diminished through the centuries.

The Church in North Africa serves as a good illustration of both missionary success and failure. The missionaries to the early Coptics translated the Bible into their language quickly and thus insured a long and vital church life. The Coptic church survives in North Africa to this day. Another group, geographically close to the Coptics, received missionaries who insisted on worship in a foreign tongue. Needless to say, the church did not prosper or continue there for long. The only reasons for this failure was the failure in communication and identification, as Nida suggests. Another failure of missionaries is the failure to communicate basic life strategies along with spiritual truths.

Nida described an experience of the early missionaries to the central Pacific in the Marshall islands. They received their mail once a year when a sailing boat made its rounds of the various islands. Nida describes it:

> On one occasion the boat was one day ahead of schedule, and the missionaries were off on a neighboring island. The captain left the mail with the Marshallese people while he attended to matters of getting stores of water and provisions. At last the Marshallese were in possession of what the missionaries spoke about so often and apparently cherished so much. The people examined the mail in order to find out what was so attractive about it. They concluded that it must be good to eat, and so they proceeded to tear all the letters into tiny bits and to cook them. However, they didn't taste very good, and the Marshallese were still puzzled about the missionaries'

strange interest in mail when the missionaries returned to find their year's correspondence made into mush."

(*Customs and Cultures*, p.5,6)

Doctrinal and ethical failure has also hounded the footsteps of missionaries through the years. The Bano'o people of the French Cammeroons shocked the first missionaries by stating, "But we want to go to hell, if it is a hot place!" The traditionally Bano'o idea of the proper place for a person after death is a hot place, without the disease producing winds. (*Customs and Cultures*, p.24) Further and more serious doctrinal error occurs when a mixture of pagan and Christian beliefs grow together. For example, in the Philippines every Easter season, men are crucified as an act of religious fervor. A missionary to Ecuador reeled in horror as he came upon a village in the north. The village people were drunk and carrying on riotously with a celebration to John the Baptist. The missionary informed the barkeeper that of all people John would have never been involved in such debauchery. The barkeeper then pointed to the mountains and said they were actually drinking to the "mountains of this valley." As Nida states, "Behind the façade of Christian cathedrals, the symbol of the cross, and the days of the saints, there still remained the ancient worship of the spirits enshrined in the mountains. The blame for these perversions lies at the feet of the mission-aries who allowed miscommunication to occur."

From this experience we see that Paul's first century exhortations to young Timothy and Titus were high orders indeed. "Teach things which befit sound doctrine..." in Titus 2:1 it is much easier said than done. For some cultures, apparently, the trans-formation may take generations. In 1Corinthians, Ephesians, Colossians and Galatians, Paul had to redeem the ethic of the twisted Greco/Roman tradi-tions, this was no less a task than what faces the missionaries of the twenty-first century.

How to teach the nations has been another sad source of failure in missions history.

For instance, the earthly authority of the church has been pressed to extremes in both Protestant and Catholic histories. In the tiny South Pacific island nation of Tonga, Methodist missionaries of the 1800's legislated spirituality for the whole of the Kingdom. After the missionaries arrived, they decreed that all idols should be destroyed. In fact, the idols were placed in boats and sent overboard deep into the Pacific. Execution repaid idolators after the decree. We are tempted to think that the spiritual vitality would have skyrocketed after this. It did — briefly. Today, although the King is a born again Christian, Mormonism is very strong in Tonga.

The history of the Papacy also affords us a rich mine of political power mongering, power brokering and the inevitable corruption that comes from absolutizing earthly political power. Peter de Rosa describes the phenomenon in the *Vicars of Christ*,

"It showed once more that it is not the unholy popes like Benedict VI who have done the most lasting damage to the church but holy ones like Gregory VII, Pius V and Pius IX. For Acton's dictum about absolute power corrupting absolutely applied, without qualification, to sinners *and* saints. In this case, Pius IX had triumphed..

What was it his Holiness had just given the force of law? The crowd's cries provided the answer: 'Viva il Papa infallible.' Pius...had invested himself with the powers of a god; he had infallibly decreed his own infallibility." (p.134)

Watching Pius invest himself with the powers of God reminds me of an article that appeared in the *Wall Street Journal* in December of 1991. The title of the article was, "Jerusalem Syndrome makes some visitors believe they're God."

JERUSALEM —

They come as tourists, hoping to sightsee and relax. But, they end up shouting prophecies from street corners, walking around naked and proclaiming themselves the Messiah.

Local psychiatrists call the phenomenon "the Jerusalem syndrome", a form of hysteria that turns 50 to 200 tourists every year, many of them previously healthy, into would-be King Davids, Virgin Marys and other Biblical figures.

'Jerusalem can literally drive some tourists crazy,' says Yair Bar-El, the director of Kfar Shaul, the government mental-health center in Jerusalem that since the early '80's, has provided psychiatric care for all foreign tourists afflicted with the illness."

As long as the church has accepted particular people as the "embodiment of God" on earth with the power to decree political and individual fates we have invariably ended up with...

"Executions multiplied. Before, there had been one or two, now there were mass burnings. Among the damned were girls of six years old. 'A bishop of Geneva', writes Lea, in the *Inquisition in the Middle Ages,* is said to have burned five hundred within three months, a bishop of Bamburg six hundred, a bishop of Wurzburg nine hundred.' So it went on. In the year 1586, the Archbishop of Treves had 118 women burned and two men for incantations that prolonged the winter." (*Vicars of Christ*)Whenever the missionary church is overcome with the "Jerusalem Syndrome" seeing itself as God's infallible or political answer, it invariably fails. We can certainly influence every part of life, including politics, just like Daniel did, but this is not our primary task, nor has God given us a promised political leadership in this world. Jesus' response to Pilate was that His Kingdom was not of *this world*. Paul and Barnabas refused to be looked at as divine in Acts 14 when the priests of Zeus wished to offer sacrifices to them.

Ultimately, the basic problem in missions failure is theological — that is — Biblical. If missionaries are living lives that are not Biblical either in ethics or doctrine, the cause — worldwide — will suffer. Macarius of Alexandria attempted to "overcome the world, the flesh and the devil" by wading into a mosquito infested marsh in Scete and dwelt there for six months. By the time he returned to his friends, they recognized him only by his voice. Unfortunately, we, like Macarius, have offered the world a twisted picture of the gospel at times, both as missionaries and as those who send out the missionaries.

In 1952, Tommy Hicks (then forty-four years of age) was conducting a series of meetings in California when God gave him a vision. While he was praying, a map of South America was spread out clearly before him. The map appeared to be covered with a vast field of golden wheat, bowed over and swaying in the breeze, ripe for harvesting. As he looked, all the stalks suddenly turned into human beings — men and women with their hands raised in the air.

They were calling to him, "Come, Brother Hicks, come and help us."

From this Macedonian call Hicks knew that God must have something special for him to do in South America, though he was still very ignorant about that part of the world. As he prayed, he felt that God was giving him a message which he scribbled down on the fly-leaf of his Bible: "For two summers will not pass over the earth until thou shalt go to this land, for thou shalt not go by boat nor by land but by bird, flying though the air thou shalt go."

Three months later, following an evangelistic crusade in California, a pastor's wife stretched out her hand toward Hicks in a prophetic prayer and, to his amazement, repeated the identical message which he had already copied into his Bible but which he had never mentioned to anyone.

As soon as he could, Tommy Hicks made arrangements to travel to South America. Though he had very little money, cash began to arrive by mail and he was now sufficiently financed to buy a one-way ticket to Buenos Aires, with about $250 to spare for his expenses. After some meetings in Temuco, Chile, before the last leg of his flight, the word "Peron" came into his mind, though he had no idea what this meant except that he felt sure that God must be speaking to him. He asked the flight attendant if she knew what it meant. "Yes", she said, "Peron is the President of Argentina!" Hicks now knew that he was on course. He must see Peron.

The missionaries who met Tommy Hicks in Buenos Aires doubted whether any such high-level meeting could possibly be arranged, especially since the President of Panama was scheduled for a state visit at that time. Finally the persistent Hicks arrived at the office of the Minister of Religion, just as his secretary appeared limping across the room toward him. Almost before he knew what he was doing, Hicks had started to pray for his healing, which came immediately. Seeing what had happened, the Minister of Religion promptly arranged an interview for him with the President himself.

When Hicks met Peron, the President was at that time suffering from eczema which so disfigured him that he allowed no personal photographs to be taken of himself. His ailment was common knowledge. Listening to Hicks tell of what the Lord wanted to do in Argentina, Peron asked him, "Can God heal me?"

Hicks replied, "Give me your hand." Right there he prayed. Peron's skin was healed instantly. Stepping back in utter amazement, he wiped his hand across his face and exclaimed in astonishment, "Dios mio, estoy curado!" (My God I am healed!)

Peron soon gave instruction that Hicks should be supplied with whatever he needed — this included the use of a large sports stadium and free access to the state radio and press.

For fifty-two days Hicks preached to an aggregate attendance of about two hundred thousand, and the Pentecostal Church in Argentina was launched into a period of very rapid church growth. The church historian Arno Enns described Hicks' campaign as "a sovereign breakthrough by God." Another influential study (W. Read et al., *Latin American Church Growth,* p.381) notes that "many evangelicals in Argentina, whether or not they agreed with Hicks' theology, admit that his meetings broke the back of the rigid resistance in Argentina to the evangelical witness there."

—David Pytches
Does God Speak Today?

CHAPTER FIVE

Missionary Successes

SUCCESS COMES IN various shapes and sizes. One of the unfortunate heresies of the 21st century church is whatever is good must be big. Scripture declares otherwise. Jesus' greatest act had a very small congregation watching. Neither Ezekiel nor Jeremiah could have written Church Growth curricula. God told both of them that no one would listen to their sermons. This was only too true! I have listened to well meaning ministers and lay people discuss the "anointing" on a ministry. Often, the "anointing" comes in numbers. "How many" go to your Church? "How many" natives were baptized in the jungle? "How many" were saved at last night's crusade? Size or speedy growth do not always equal success in missionary efforts. Baptist Pastor, Ronnie Floyd writes that he gave up the idol of numbers of Baptisms as his relationship with the Lord grew (he pastors a church of 10,000). Many missionaries have labored for years with small reports for the "how many" mongers. Many have died on harsh fields, with no one wanting to write their biographies, and no one interviewing them for "church growth" seminars. Yet, they have been faithful like Jeremiah and Ezekiel were in their day. As we look at the issue of "how many" and what missionary success really is, we must not overlook how God has used missionaries in Korea.

In 1981, my wife and I sat at lunch with Dr. J. Edwin Orr. Orr knew more about revivals and the history of revivals than anyone in the 20th century. Fuller Seminary employed him to teach about it. Judy and I were preparing to go to Korea for our first time. Knowing about the numbers of conversions and numbers of Christians there, I thought this would be a great opportunity to ask the leading authority on revival about the "Korean Revival." Orr responded, "I believe Korea is an example of a whole nation turning to Christ." At that time the estimated percentage of truly repentant Christians in the population was 30%. Judy and I were excited to be there and see what God was doing. To say that it was "breath taking" is an understatement. When I went to a rather high hill in the middle of the city of Seoul, the prominent feature of the landscape was the large numbers of plain white crosses atop church buildings in every direction as far as I could see.

Our ears were also impacted by the church in Korea. Morning by morning we were awakened by Christians singing. The saints arose around 4 a.m. to start the morning prayer meetings. Christians began this around the turn of the century and it has continued for ninety years.

Presbyterians are the dominant church culture in Korea. Several of the largest churches in the world are there. The Full Gospel Church on Yoido Island stops traffic each Sunday morning (over 500,000 tithing members attend several packed services.) Korea changed my life and Judy's life by giving us a new perspective on what God can do in a nation.

However, this phenomenon in Korea can lead us to wrong conclusions. Some Christians declare, "If the rest of the church prayed like Koreans, they would see this kind of vitality also." Or, "If everyone met in small groups like Pastor Cho's Full Gospel Church, their church would grow like wild fire, as well." Many people do not know the rich heritage of the Korean Church.

How did the phenomenal "sudden" Korean church growth occur? Rotting bones of hundreds of martyred missionaries tell the "success story" of Korean Christianity. Kenneth Scott Latourette describes the first major thrust of the gospel into Korea.

"It appears not to have been until 1784, or on the eve of the nineteenth century, that Christianity began a continuing life in Korea...Persecution by the state was the lot of the Christians almost from the first. An important cause of the opposition was the refusal of the converts to take part in the ancestral cult, for this, as in China, appeared to strike at the very basis of morality and society. There was also the fear that the Christian groups, meeting clandestinely, might, like secret societies, be nuclei of sedition and rebellion. Probably, too, the proscription of Christianity by both Korea's great neighbors, and particularly by China, contributed to the official attitude. Before the end of the century, there were a number of martyrdoms...

By that time the Christians were said to have numbered several thousand...The persecution...is reported to have cost several hundred lives...most of the Christians of any social or political importance were dead or in exile and the Church seemed on the way to extinction." (*A History of the Expansion of Christianity,* Kenneth Scott Latourette, Volume 6, p.416, 417) Latourette states that another violent persecution broke out in 1866 and another one in 1881 which again threatened the church with extinction (Ibid, p.418).

Don Richardson wrote in 1981, "Every day in South Korea an average of 10 new Protestant churches open their doors for the first time to accommodate the still-rising flood of converts."

For almost 200 years and possibly more, God has

been working in Korea in a large part, because of anonymous martyrs who faithfully served God in the 1700's. These unknown martyrs were just as "successful" in their small missions endeavors as the pastors of the contemporary "mega" churches of 20th century Korea. We are tempted to think that the modern day Koreans are successful only because of their small groups or prayer practices when, in reality, their success has come with a very high and brutal historical price tag. Christians labored in obscurity, suffered persecution and died faithful-hideously faithful-vicious deaths. Like Abraham, they looked for a city whose builder and maker was God. These Korean missionaries and saints were like those mentioned in Hebrews 11 "of whom the world was not worthy."

In the early 1900's an unknown Singaporean pastor succeeded with one young man. This success with one person turned out to have a radical and delayed impact on the whole body of Christ in that city of 3 million. The story begins a few years earlier in China.

An evangelist named Tang and his family traveled throughout part of China evangelizing and planting churches. The persecution forced the elderly Tang to send his son south through the Malaysian peninsula to Singapore where he could find a new and more peaceful life. Young C.K. Tang arrived in Singapore at twenty-three years old. He owned a tin cup and a small piece of lace. He looked for work and a place to live. Finding neither for a considerable period of time, C.K. approached the unknown pastor about his need for a place to stay. The pastor told Tang that he could sleep in the church sanctuary until he found a job and a place to live. As time progressed, Tang found a job and a small place to live. On the last morning of his stay in that pastor's church, Tang told the Lord he would one day build Him a church if he ever obtained the financial means to do it. This was to say thank you to God for the kindness of that pastor.

Time passed and Tang became fabulously wealthy as a businessman with interests in several markets. After Tang turned eighty years old, he desired to fulfill his vow to the Lord, which he had made as a young man.

The Church of Our Savior in Singapore was looking for a new sanctuary to worship in because it had grown so much in the early '80's. Tang heard of the need and bought an old theatre that the Church of Our Savior wanted for their new building. Tang paid cash for the building —over 1 million Singapore dollars (about 75,000 U.S.D.). The day he wrote out the check, God healed him of a long-standing painful illness. The Church of Our Savior has started over 20 churches in other parts of the world and gives literally multiplied thousands of dollars to the work of evangelism around the world every year. The blessing of a new building occurred because an unknown pastor showed kindness to a needy young Chinese man named C.K.Tang! That is missionary success—showing kindness to one person! By so doing "some have entertained angels unaware", says the writer to the Hebrews.

One recent edition of *Charisma* magazine discussed the current sweep of the Holy Spirit in Latin America. *Christianity Today*, April 5, 1992 also ran an edition with the cover story titled, "Why is Latin America turning Protestant?" The articles discussed the contemporary move of God in the churches in Mexico, Guatemala, Brazil, Chile, Argentina and Venezuela. The articles focused on the work, among others, of Carlos Annacondia and Claudio Freidzon in Argentina. The *Charisma* article tells of over 2 million reported conversions in Annacondia's meetings and thousands simultaneously converted in Freidzon's meetings. I have been in a Claudio Freidzon meeting. It was one of the more powerful services I have been privileged to witness. As we consider this movement, we dishonor the church if we forget the "successful others" who preceded the present era: D. H. Wheeler who was martyred in 1856 circulating the Scriptures in Central America, Mr. and Mrs. Thomas Pond who arrived in Caracas, Venezuela, in 1897 and started a Presbyterian work, the untold story of David Trumbull in Chile around 1855, R. Nesbit died in 1857 in the upper Amazon region of

Brazil passing out copies of Scripture to the Brazilians. (See Latourette, *History of the Expansion of Christianity*, Vol. 5) All of these people were "successful" as missionaries and contributed to the present move of God in South America by laying sacrificial, violent and martyred foundations.

As I stated, "success" comes in different shapes and sizes. My sister-in-law, Janet, went to Hong Kong in 1981 with an outreach team. She found thousands of refugees living in sub-human conditions. Loren Cunningham describes Janet's place of missionary "success."

…The first refugee camp we visited was in Hong Kong. No magazine articles could prepare eyes and ears—or nose—for the shock of that scene in Camp Jubilee.

The smell came first. The brown stench of raw human waste hit us before we entered the place. As we walked in the main entrance, into an inner passageway, we found the source. The lower floor of the building was eight inches deep in human waste. We picked our way around the perimeter as best we could, camp officials pointing to some broken sewer pipes along the side of the wall. There was not enough money to hire a plumber from the city and no one there was qualified or willing to tackle the huge mess.

Jubilee Camp was a former police barracks designed to hold 900. Now the condemned structure held 8,000…" (*Is That Really You, God?,* Loren Cunningham, p.141,142)

Janet wrote her mother asking for hip boots (fisherman style waders) and perfume. Janet shoveled and snorted her perfume drenched arm band for days until the refugee camp became livable and reasonably sanitary again. It is interesting to note that in Cunningham's book, he wrote that no one was "willing to tackle the mess." Remarkably, winning in the spiritual war sometimes means simply showing up for the contest and being "willing" to get your hands dirty—literally!

Church history is replete with other successful and largely unknown women missionaries—literally from A-Z — such as: Eliza Agnew served in Ceylon for forty years in the mid 1840's (lived to 76). Lulu Bookwalter was a school administrator for 30 years in Ceylon (now Sri Lanka) (lived to 75). Louise Campbell founded the Kwong Yet Missionary School and was the first single woman missionary to serve in south China for 40 years, (lived to 85). Lillian Dickson went to Taiwan to establish 183 kindergartens and 200 churches in various countries until her death in 1983, (lived to 82). In the late 1800's, Mary Edwards established the Inanda Seminary for women in Zululand, where she worked for 57 years with only one furlough to the United States (lived to 98). Elizabeth Falck worked as a nurse and taught English from 1921-1951 in Shanghai. She moved to

Tokyo and taught for eight years until her retirement from missions (lived to 86). Christine Garnett worked in Cuba for 46 years starting an orphanage, a girl's school and an old folks' home, (lived to 86). Lillian Hamer worked as a nurse in China and Thailand where she was murdered at the age of 47, in 1959, by the tribal people to whom she was ministering. Marilla Ingalls ministered for 40 years in Burma, establishing the Bible Society there, (lived to 65). Minnie James wrote program materials for the Women's Missionary Society in the Southern Baptist church for 40 years, (lived to 89). Florence Keller was the doctor of the Maori royal family and a missionary doctor among the Maoris in New Zealand for 47 years, (lived to 99). Lydia Lehman ministered in India for 24 years as a Mennonite missionary, (lived to 85).

Nellie Okken worked until 1983 as a medical missionary to Zaire, completing 39 years of missionary service, (lived to 68). Dr. Ruth Parmelee worked as a medical relief missionary in Turkey and Greece from 1914-1973, (lived to 88). Mary Reed worked 52 years among the Mission to Lepers in India, contracted leprosy herself (lived to 88). Katharina Schellenberg served as medical missionary for the Mennonites in India for 38 years in India during the early 1900's, (lived to 75). Lucy Thurston pioneered a missions project in Kona, Hawaii, in 1820 together with her husband and she remained there 56 years, (lived to 81). Lillias Underwood worked as a medical missionary to Korea for 28 years, (lived to 67). Dr. Harriet Vaughan founded women's, children's and leper's hospitals in Madura, South India and worked there over 20 years, (lived to 86). Mary Whatley went to Egypt at 32 years old and stayed until she was in her 60's, establishing schools, hospitals and teaching (lived to 65). Annie Yeo worked as Mennonite missionary among the Nupe people in Nigeria for 33 years, influencing many youth, (lived to 79). (*A Dictionary of Women in Church History*, Mary L. Hammack)

T.L. Osborn and Reinhard Bonnke have both witnessed tremendous moves of God in Africa with literally thousands of healings and churches started out of their crusades. A Kenyan friend told me that Osborn could fill any stadium in the nation of Kenya with 250,000 people night after night with only 3 days advance notice to the town or city to which he went. We hear repeatedly that Billy Graham has spoken personally to more people than any person in history. My opinion is that T.L. Osborn is either close to that same place of honor or has surpassed it. Osborn is less well-known in the west, particularly in America, but has had impact in Africa and Asia that is mind-boggling! Ghana opened up to the gospel as a result of the direct ministry of Osborn's wife, Daisy, to the President of Ghana. Osborn and his wife have ministered to Yoyeri Museveni in Uganda.

Uganda, like Ghana, is wide open to Osborn's evangelistic efforts.

Osborn's writing ministry is also mind-boggling. When he prints books to give away at his evangelistic crusades, he prints as many as a million copies. One friend of mine in Asia who oversees a ministry gave away a million tracts during a Christmas outreach. Those million tracts had been donated free from Osborn's ministry.

Judy and I traveled to Uganda during the summer of 1992. We went there because we had been involved in starting Bible schools in four Africa nations. We visited two of them when we were there, Kenya and Uganda. We fell in love with Uganda and its people. It is understandable why the British called Uganda the "Pearl of Africa". The natural beauty is overwhelming in spite of the pain the nation has endured for the last 30 years. As I left the nation to go to Kenya, I saw a very kind looking lady sitting in the restaurant security section. So, I began to walk over to her and speak with her, but she beat me to it. She invited me to sit down and she bought me a coke. Her name was May Dodzweit. She told me that she had been a missionary in East Africa for thirty years. I asked her to send me her newsletter describing her ministry. Here is part of her letter, describing her earlier work:

"We had established 3,000 congregations in East and Central Africa. 2,000 in Zaire (former Beglian

Congo), 300 in Burundi, about the same in Rwanda, and about the same in Western Tanzania and 500 here in Uganda. Now there are about 600 here and 3,000 in Zaire. The nationals are doing most of the work and I am involved in administration mostly and teaching in Sunday School and VBS work in Kampala. I also coordinate seminars and large Crusades with other church groups and among other churches. To define my work is hard to do because there are so many different things I am directly or indirectly involved in."

She writes in another letter, "God is moving by His Spirit. One of our largest works is in Kinshasa, Zaire, (former Leopoldville, Congo), where there are over 100 congregations numbering 25,000 or more Christians. The largest building we have in that city at the present time only crowds in a bit over 2,000, but outside speakers enable the hundreds and sometimes thousands outside, to enjoy the service." (Personal letters, Fall of 1992)

May Dodzweit has been "successful" in Uganda. The missionary martyrs (Hannington and others) between 1870 and 1900 were also "successful" in Uganda.

The book of Acts teaches us that nothing can stop God's Word. On August 13, 1727, God filled the whole community of Moravians at Herrnhut in Germany with the Holy Spirit. This ignited a missionary fire that propelled them around the world. The onward march of the Word continued.

We need to pray for the church that God will do for us what He did for the Moravians and to follow the example of D. L. Moody in Northfield, Massachusetts, as described by R. A. Torrey.

"At three o'clock we gathered in front of Mr. Moody's mother's home; four hundred and fifty-six of us in all, all men from the eastern colleges. We commenced to climb the mountainside. After we had gone some distance Mr. Moody said: 'I do not think we need to go further. Let us stop here. I can see no reason why we should not kneel down here now and ask God that the Holy Spirit may fall on us as definitely as He fell on the Apostles at Pentecost. Let us pray.' We knelt down on the ground; some of us lay on our faces on the pine-needles. The Holy Ghost fell upon us. It was a wonderful hour. There are many who will never forget it." (*The Person and Work of the Holy Spirit*, R. A. Torrey, D.D.) From that little town of Northfield, Massachusetts, prayer power sent out waves and waves of missionaries to the uttermost parts of the world, some paying for their missions commitment with their own lives.

CHAPTER SIX

Missionary Pain

PLEASE DON'T JUDGE this story according to moral standards! Just receive the facts! The two daughters of a Christian martyr - Christians themselves, became prostitutes to support their smaller brothers and sick mother. Their younger brother of fourteen became mad when he saw it and had to be put in an asylum. When, after years, the imprisoned father returned, his only prayer was, "God take me again to prison. I cannot bear to see this." His prayer has been fulfilled and he is now in jail again for the crime of having witnessed for Christ to children. His daughters are no longer prostitutes. They have received jobs by complying with the demands of the secret police. They have become informers. As daughters of a Christian martyr, they are received with honor in every house. They listen and then they report everything they hear to the secret police. (*Tortured for Christ*, Richard Wurmbrand)

Torture comes in various forms for missionaries. Through the centuries, God-haters have devised many diabolical methods. The Apostle Paul focused on seven tortures:

1. The Arena
2. Crucifixion
3. The Sword
4. Stoning
5. Burning
6. Prison
7. Beatings

(*Persecution and Martyrdom in the Theology of Paul*, John S. Pobee, p. 1-13)

1. THE ARENA:

Bloodthirsty Romans watched starving wild animals attack their victims. These victims suffered greatly, often being tied to a stake and then devoured. At other times, they were allowed a weapon to defend themselves, only to prolong the show and the torture. Robbery, murder, sacrilege and arson earned a person center stage in the arena. In I Corinthians 4, Paul compared the first century apostles to these criminals. Pobee states that there were 270 such arenas all over the empire during the first century. Paul also alludes to this where he discusses having fought the "beasts of Ephesus."

2. CRUCIFIXION:

Peter and his brother, Andrew, both died this way. Peter was crucified upside down and Andrew was placed into the ground side-ways like an "X". "Originally merely a stake on which the victim was tied or impaled, by Roman times the cross featured a horizontal beam, placed either at the top of the vertical shaft (in the form of the Greek letter T, St. Anthony's Cross) or slightly below the top (the traditional Latin cross). The later "Greek" cross comprised vertical and horizontal bars of equal length, the X shaped St. Anthony's cross also was employed later in Roman times. Judging from first century A.D. remains from a tomb near Jerusalem, it appears that the victim's feet were pierced with a single nail, which was then driven into a small olivewood board (to keep the feet together) but not into the upright shaft itself. The forearms were nailed to the horizontal bar. A small horizontal board was affixed to the cross at buttocks thereby prolonging the suffering. One might agonize on the cross for several days before dying, apparently of suffocation. Thirst was intense and the weight of the body produced inexorable pain; victims were tormented by high fever and convulsions, which racked their entire body. Occasionally the executioners prompted death by breaking the victim's bones.

As further humiliation for the victim and as a deterrent to potential offenders, the person condemned to crucifixion was first flogged, then ordered to carry a horizontal crossbeam to the place of execution, where it was hoisted onto the vertical pole".

(*Eerdman's Bible Dictionary*, p.246)

3. THE SWORD:

Romans viewed Christians as apostates and cannibals. This "apostasy" and "cannibalism" invited the Roman sword of execution. Paul died this way in 64 A.D. by the order of the bi-sexual crazed emperor, Nero.

Nero was later declared to be "god." Under Nero, the military used the sword on criminals and Christians, and, in fact, this was a common practice. In other parts of the empire, the axe head severed the criminal's head from his neck. Paul mentions the sword in Romans 8:35.

4. STONING:

The Jews practiced stoning. The Romans allowed them to do it in certain instances throughout the first century. In Acts 14, Paul suffered stoning at the hands of Jewish zealots.

Usually, the criminal dug his own grave about 3 feet by 9 feet square and about 6 to 9 feet deep. The Jewish officials tied his hands to his side and pushed him backwards into his own grave. Often, the fall would break the neck of the criminal, killing him when he hit the bottom of the grave. Stones were simply piled on top of him. The witness threw the first stone. They also aimed their first stones at the heart of the criminal because the Jews held that crime and sin originated in the human heart. The root of the problem must be dealt with! Apparently Paul did not dig his own grave in Acts 14. If he did, Luke omitted much of the story.

Paul witnessed another stoning in Acts 7. Stephen was not as fortunate as Paul.

5. BURNING:

After Nero burned Rome in 64 A.D., he blamed the Christians. The Roman historian Tacitus writes: "Nero fabricated scapegoats — punished with every refinement the notoriously depraved Christians (as they were popularly called). Their originator, Christ, had been executed in Tiberius' reign by the governor of Judea, Pontius Pilatus.

First, Nero had self-acknowledged Christians arrested. Then on their information, large numbers of others were condemned — not so much for incendiarism as for their anti-social tendencies. Their deaths were made farcical. Dressed in wild animals' skins, they were torn to pieces by dogs, or crucified, or made into torches to be ignited after dark as substitutes for daylight. Nero provided his gardens for the spectacle, and exhibited displays in the Circus, at which he mingled with the crowd —

or stood in a chariot, dressed as a charioteer. Despite their guilt as Christians, and the ruthless punishment it deserved, the victims were pitied. For it was felt that they were being sacrificed to one man's brutality rather than to the national interest."

(*The Annals of Tacitus*, Penguin Classics, p.365,366)

6. IMPRISONMENT

Paul and many of the first century Christians experienced various forms of imprisonment. Some far more humane and just than others. Reading through Paul's letters we find imprisonment mentioned in Romans, Corinthians, Ephesians, Colossians, Philippians, 2 Timothy and Philemon.

7. BEATING:

Paul faced Roman floggings and Jewish lashings (2 Cor.11:24). Some Roman floggings were for warning others or to punish for offenses already committed. They varied in fierceness. Non-Roman citizens could get severe floggings with whips laced with razor sharp glass, bone or metals. Such scourgings were sometimes fatal. Jewish lashings were more humane and measured with forty being the highest number, reduced to thirty-nine by the rabbis.

Many Christians have never considered a crucial selling point about the Word of God. Most of the New Testament writers died violent deaths. They believed in what they wrote so completely, that they could have autographed their books with their own blood. I wrote how New Testament characters died next to the title of their book in one of my older Bibles. I will let you look over my shoulder as I leaf through some of its pages.

- Matthew — Flayed to death with a long shaft-ed axe.
- Mark — Dragged to death.
- Luke — Hung upside down on an olive tree.
- John — Boiled in oil — but supernaturally delivered!
- Paul — Beheaded.
- Timothy — Beat to death.
- James — Stoned to death.
- Peter— Crucified upside down.

One of the apostle John's great grandchildren in the faith was Polycarp. The martyrdom of Polycarp has galvanized the church through the centuries. Lightfoot and Harmer quote it in their discussion of *The Apostolic Fathers*, Baker, p.138ff

"But as Polycarp entered the stadium, there came a voice from heaven:"Be strong Polycarp, and act like a man." And no one saw the speaker, but those of our people who were present heard the voice. And then, as he was brought forward, there was a great tumult when they heard that Polycarp had been arrested. Therefore, when he was brought before him, the proconsul asked if he were Polycarp. And when he confessed that he was, the proconsul tried to persuade him to recant, saying, "Have respect for your age," and other things as they are accustomed to say: "Swear by the genius of Caesar; repent; say, "Away with the Atheists!" So, Polycarp solemnly looked at the whole crowd of lawless heathen who were in the stadium, motioned toward them with his hand, and then (groaning as he looked up to heaven) said, "Away with the Athiests!" But when the magistrate persisted and said, "Swear the oath, and I will release you; revile Christ," Polycarp replied, "For eighty-six years I have been his servant, and he has done me no wrong. How can I blaspheme the King who saved me?"

"When he had offered up the "Amen" and finished his prayer, the men in charge lit the fire. And as a mighty flame blazed up we saw a miracle (we that is, to whom it was given to see), and we have been preserved in order that we might tell the rest what happened. For the fire taking the shape of an arch, like sail of a ship filled by the wind, completely surround the body of the martyr; and it was there in the middle, not like flesh burning but like bread baking or like gold and silver being refined in a furnace. For we also perceived a very fragrant odor, as if it were the scent of incense or some other precious spice.

"When the lawless men eventually realized that

his body could not be consumed by fire, they ordered an executioner to go up to him and stab him with a dagger. And when he did this, there came out a large quantity of blood, so that it extinguished the fire; and the whole crowd was amazed that there should be so great a difference between the unbelievers and the elect."

Church history records other fatal consequences for faithfulness. John the Baptist's decapitation truly prophesied that faithful messengers do lose their lives. Unfortunately, church history is replete with carnage. Doubly unfortunate is the self-inflicted carnage of one bearing Christ's name literally martyring another. God must weep over this. The most dynamic missionary movement in church history started this way — the Moravians.

The Moravians—spiritual grandchildren of John Hus—covered the face of the earth in the 1700's. How did Hus die in the 1500's? His story is grievous. "On the morning of July 6 Hus was ushered into the cathedral of Constance in Bohemia ... Hus was placed upon a high stool in the middle of the huge building. The bishop of Lodi (in Czechoslovakia) preached a funeral sermon saying that the blotting out of heretics was one of the works most pleasing to God. Thirty charges of heresy were read and when Hus attempted to speak, he was ordered to remain silent. At length, the proceeding came to an end. Attendants placed upon Hus' head a tall fool's cap decorated with a picture of three devils fighting for his soul, and the march to the place of execution began. A thousand soldiers cleared the way. As the procession passed the city square, Hus saw the huge bonfire in which copies of his books were being burned. To this stake Hus was bound with wet ropes. Then straw and wood were piled up around him. Once more he was asked if he would recant. " I shall die with joy," he replied, "in the faith of the gospel which I have preached."

An officer clapped his hands and the burning torch was applied to the straw. As the flames flared up around him, Hus began to sing in Latin one of the chants of the church: "Christ, Thou Son Of the Living God, have mercy upon me!" And so, upon "a chariot of fire" the soul of John Hus went up to heaven. When the fire had consumed the martyr's body, soldiers gathered up the ashes and tossed them into the Rhine, so that friends might find nothing which could be kept as a relic of the man." *Through Five Hundred Years: A Popular History of the Moravian Church*, Allen W. Schattschneider, (p.15,16)

The Moravian church was born that day! Who was the cruel mid-wife? Peter de Rosa, Professor of Ethics at Westminster Theological Seminary, gives us a dark background to the death of Hus. In his revealing book, *The Vicars of Christ, A History of the Dark Side of the Papacy*, (p.94ff), de Rosa describes the council which condemned Hus to the martyr's death.

"When the clergy met in large numbers, it was always wise to choose a town near water — lake or river — for disposing of the bodies. Lake Constance received over five hundred while the Council was in session; the Rhine, too, hid many secrets. Another requirement was that the meeting-place had to be large enough to accommodate the vast number of prostitutes who found the clergy required their services more urgently than the military and paid keener prices. At the height of the Council (which condemned Hus to death), there were reckoned to be over twelve hundred whores in Constance working around the clock.

It was a massive gathering, including three hundred bishops, three hundred top theologians and the cardinals of all three obediences."

The unrighteous death of Hus helped springboard a Bible movement throughout Europe, which culminated in Martin Luther — who greatly influenced the later Moravians. This one death, the death of Hus, produced later Moravian missionaries in: Denmark, St. Croix, St. Thomas, St. John, The Grand Cayman Islands, Jamaica, Antigua, Barbados, St. Kitts, Trinidad, Tobago, Guyana, Greenland, North American Indians, Surinam, South Africa, Kenya, Tanzania, Labrador, England, Russia, Nicaragua, Honduras, Australia, Northwest India, Alaska, Israel, Lebanon, Transjordan, Ireland, Scotland, Wales, Sweden, Poland, Latvia, Prussia, Switzerland, Czechoslovakia and the list goes on and on!" (Ibid, Schattschneider)

Little did the Council of Constance realize on that July day in 1415 that their act was prophetic. After they burned Hus at the stake, they scattered his ashes in the Rhine River. This scattering was only a picture of the way God would one day take his spiritual descendants and literally scatter them over the whole earth preaching the gospel that Hus preached!

Carnage produced consecration world-wide!

Lest we think that Christians torturing Christians has been an isolated event, we must look briefly at the inquisition as distasteful as it was. The most famous of all inquisitors was Thomas of Torquemada who ruled tyrannically in religious matters in the 1480's, also known simply as "Torquemada." His victims of torture for "heresy" numbered over 114,000 of whom "10, 220 were burned." (de Rosa, p.170)

We can look at the persecution of Elvira del Campo. She was charged with being a "Jew". Official proceeding began against her on April 6, 1568, carried out by Dominicans and an Episcopal vicar. They warned her that she would be tortured unless she came out with the whole truth as to her Jewishness or not.

They carried her to the torture-chamber and

stripped her naked. They gave her a small pair of trunks to cover her shame. They tied her arms and twisted the cords painfully. She told them she did not eat pork because it made her sick. They then placed her on a trestle with her head lower than her feet and sharp edges digging into the back of her body. The cords on her limbs were then tightened. They shoved an iron prong into her mouth and thrust a piece of linen into her throat. She begged for mercy saying that she was strangling."

DeRosa writes:

Slowly, the executioner poured water from a quart jar onto the linen, allowing it to drip down her throat. Some prisoners had six to eight jars poured down them and suffocated as a result. Elvira tried to say she was dying when the linen was removed, she was silent, either because she had nothing to say or because she was unable to speak. The torture was suspended for four days. From then on her speech was mostly incoherent.

In the end, the inquisitors managed to elicit from her that her refusal to eat pork and her Saturday change of clothes was proof of her Judaism. Once she realized what was required of her, she was relieved to admit her apostasy and plead for mercy.

One judge was for burning her. Elvira was not burned. Her property was confiscated, she was ordered to wear the robe of shame; she was sentenced to serve three more years in prison. For some reason, perhaps insanity, she was released after six months. The case was closed. A devout Christian, she was imprisoned and tortured without mercy by the pope's representatives in the pope's name!" (Ibid, p.168ff) Christians can, at times, indeed be as cruel to each other as the world is to us. Christians killing each other is not limited to Catholics killing Protestants. Protestants have also killed each other. The history of the Anabaptists is unfortunate testimony to this. No doubt, in Northern Ireland Protestants have also killed Catholics.

The unbelieving world has always opposed us and always will. Blandina died the martyr's death in Lyons, France, in 177 A.D. She was a female slave who endured torture before her death. Her murderers hung her on a post as bait for wild animals. The torturers finally unleashed a bull on her who killed her after she had been burned with a hot griddle and attacked by other wild animals.

Crispina of North Africa challenges our faith. In the year 304 A.D. the Roman Emporer Diocletian had Crispina's head severed for her testimony, after she refused to offer a sacrifice to the Roman gods. As well, Diocletian ordered all church buildings to be leveled, copies of the Scriptures to be burned. As well, all Christians were removed from high government offices. He imprisoned bishops. He released them if they compromised their faith. (*Encyclope-*

dia of Early Christianity, p.256)

Everett Ferguson from Abilene Christian University writes that there were four martyrs in the early church with the same name — "Dasius."

Nothing much is known about how they died, except for one who was killed during the pagan celebration of Saturnalia by Roman soldiers. The early writer, Tertullian, wrote that some people were converted to Christianity by the faithful witness of the martyrs. Hippolytus was an early bishop and martyr in Rome who died around 236 A.D. Fox mentions this, as well, in his Book of Martyrs about the killing of Andrew, Simon Peter's brother. While Andrew hung sideways on his cross, he continued preaching the gospel and many were saved by his testimony from the cross. Anastasius of Antioch was mutilated and burned in the midst of a time of Jewish persecution of the church in 610 A.D.

The martyrdom of Potamiana and Basilides was the first recorded incidence of saints having boiling pitch poured on them for their faith in Christ. Egypt set the stage — it was the year 210 A.D. Basilides had a vision three nights before Potamiana was to be executed. Basilides was the soldier ordered to lead her to the place of death. He dutifully obeyed the order and then was killed also. He had been converted three nights earlier because of the vision he had received about Potamiana!

Perpetua and Felicitas died in 203 A.D. in North

Africa. They both died in the arena after Perpetua had received four visions. Two of these visions encouraged them in their faith in Christ.

Pliny, governor for the Emperor Trajan stated that: "A great many individuals of every age and class, both men and women, are being brought to trial, and this is likely to continue." (Pliny the Younger)

We could continue on and on with ancient accounts of torture and death. The twentieth century proved to be one of the most deadly for Christians. In fact, some people believe we now live in the most deadly century for Christians.

Richard Wurmbrand spent fourteen years in a communist jail in Romania. He describes some of the tortures he saw there.

"A pastor by the name of Florescu was tortured with red-hot iron pokers and with knives. He was beaten very badly. Then starving rats were driven into his cell through a large pipe. He could not sleep, but had to defend himself all the time. If he rested for a moment, the rats would attack him.

He was forced to stand for two weeks, day and night. The communists wished to compel him to betray his brethren, but he resisted steadfastly. In the end, they brought his fourteen year old son and began to whip the boy in front of his father, saying that they would continue to beat him until the pastor said what they wished him to say. The poor man was half mad. He bore it as long as he could. When he could not stand it any more, he cried to his son, "Alexander, I must say what they want! I can't bear your beating anymore!" The son answered, "Father, don't do me the injustice to have a traitor as a parent. Withstand! If they kill me, I will die with the words, "Jesus and my fatherland." The communists, enraged, fell upon the child and beat him to death, with blood spattered over the walls of the cell. He died praising God. Our dear brother Florescu was never the same after seeing this.

Handcuffs, which had sharp nails on the insides were put on our wrists. If we were totally still, they didn't cut us. But, in bitterly cold cells, when we shook with cold, our wrists would be torn by the nails.

Christians were hung upside down on ropes and beaten so severely that their bodies swung back and forth under the blows. Christians were put in ice-box "refrigerator cells" which were so cold, frost and ice covered the inside. I was thrown into one with very little clothing on. Prison doctors would watch through an opening until they saw symptoms of freezing to death. They would give a warning and guards would rush in to take us out and make us warm. When we were finally warmed, we would immediately be put back in the ice-box cells to freeze — over and over again! Thawing out, then freezing to within just one minute or two of death, then being thawed out again. It continued endlessly. Even today sometimes I can't bear to open a refrigerator.

We Christians were put in wooden boxes only slightly larger than we were. This left no room to move. Dozens of sharp nails were driven into every side of the box, with their razor-sharp point sticking into the box. While we stood perfectly still, it was alright. We were forced to stand in these boxes for endless hours. But, when we became fatigued and swayed with tiredness, the nails would go into our bodies. If we moved or twitched a muscle, there were horrible nails." (*Tortured for Christ*, p.36ff)

Wurmbrand relates a story about how he calls "one of the really great heroes of the faith". It was Pastor Milan Haimovici.

The prisons were overcrowded and the guards did not know us by name. They called out for those who had been sentenced to get twenty-five lashes with a whip for having broken some prison rule. Innumerable times, Pastor Milan Haimovici went to get the beating in the place of somebody else. By this he won the respect of other prisoners for not only himself, but also for Christ whom he represented.

If I were to continue to tell all the horrors of communists and all the self-sacrifices of Christians, I would never finish.

One of our workers was a young girl of the

Underground church. The communist police discovered that she secretly spread gospels and taught children about Christ. They decided to arrest her. But, to make the arrest more agonizing and as painful as they could, they decided to delay her arrest a few weeks until the day she was to be married. On her wedding day, the girl was dressed as a bride. The most wonderful, joyous day in a girl's life! Suddenly, the door was pushed open and the secret police rushed in. When the bride saw the secret police, she held out her arms toward them to be handcuffed. They roughly put the manacles on her wrists. She looked toward her beloved, then kissed the chains and said, "I thank my heavenly Bridegroom for this jewel He has presented to me on my marriage day. I thank Him that I am worthy to suffer for Him." She was dragged off. Weeping Christians and a weeping bridegroom were left behind. They knew what happens to young Christian girls in the hands of communist guards. After five years she was released — a destroyed, broken woman looking thirty years older. Her bridegroom had waited for her. She said it was the least she could do for Christ. (Ibid p. 40)

Wurmbrand states: "The tortures and brutality continued without interruption. When I lost consciousness or became too dazed to give the torturers any further hopes of confessions, I would be returned to my cell. There I would lie, untended and half dead, to regain a little strength so they could work on me again. Many died at this stage, but somehow my strength always managed to come back. In the ensuing year, in several different prisons, they broke four vertebrae in my back, and many other bones. They carved me in a dozen places. They burned and cut eighteen holes in my body.

Doctors in Oslo, seeing all this and the scars of the lung tuberculosis, which I also had, declared that my being alive today is a pure miracle! According to their medical books, I should have been dead for years. I know myself it is a miracle. God is a God of miracles." (Ibid p.41)

Wurmbrand further recalls, "In the prison of Gherla, a Christian named Grecu was sentenced to be beaten to death. The process lasted a few weeks. He was beaten very slowly. He would be hit once at the bottom of the feet with a rubber club, and then left. After some minutes again a hit, after another few minutes again. He was beaten on the testicles. Then a doctor gave him an injection. He recovered and was given very good food to restore his strength, and then he was beaten again until he died under this slow, repeated beating. One who led this torture was a member of the Central Committee of the Communist Party, whose name was Reck." (Ibid p.44) Reck was later converted to Christianity!

What happened to the families who took in

Wurmbrand's son while his father and mother were in prison? Wurmbrand states: "It was a crime to help families of Christian martyrs, Two ladies who helped him were arrested and beaten so badly that they are crippled even now — after fifteen years. A lady who risked her life and took Mihai (Wurmbrand's son) into her house was sentenced to eight years in prison for the crime of having helped families of prisoners. All her teeth were kicked out. Her bones were broken. She will never be able to work again. She, too, will be a cripple for life." (Ibid P.48)

Missionary doctor to Zaire (Africa), Helen Roseveare relates her story: "Someone else had to carry your workload on top of theirs. Why did I keep getting ill? Was I just becoming a burden to the team? Would it be better if I went home? Then during the rebellion on the night of October 28, 1964, cruel men broke into my home around midnight. It was a wicked, savage night. I had tried to escape from them. What a hope! Six soldiers, armed and with powerful flash lights, surrounded the house and moved in on me as on a trapped animal. Numbed and terrified, I lay in the mud beneath a meager hedge. Pulled roughly to my feet, I was struck across the face. My glasses went and my nose was gashed and bleeding. A second blow felled me to the ground where the leader's boot crashed cruelly into my face and then my ribs. My back teeth were broken, my whole body bruised. I was driven back to the verandah of my home, jeered at, cursed and insulted. My benumbed brain was only able to keep me one step ahead of them, one inch out of reach of each succeeding lunge. I wasn't praying. I was beyond praying. Someone back home was earnestly praying for me. If I had prayed any prayer, it would have been, "My God, my God, why has Thou forsaken me?" Suddenly there was a God. I didn't see any vision or hear a voice, but I just knew with every ounce of my being that God was actually vitally there — God, in all his majesty and power. And he stretched his arms out to me, surrounding me with love, and seemed to whisper, "Twenty years ago you asked me for the privilege of being a missionary. This is it. Don't you want it?" Fantastic. The privilege of being identified with our Savior. As I was driven down the short corridor of my home, it was as though He clearly said to me, "These are not your sufferings. They are not beating you. These are my sufferings. All I ask of you is the loan of your body."

An enormous relief swept through me, one word became unbelievably clear. That word was privilege. He did not take away pain or cruelty or humiliation. No, it was all there, but now it was altogether different. It was with Him, for Him, in Him. He was actually offering me the inestimable privilege of sharing in some little way in the fellowship of His sufferings.

In the weeks of imprisonment that followed and

in the subsequent year of continued service, I have looked back and tried to 'count the cost', but I find it all swallowed by in privilege. The cost suddenly seems very small and transient in the greatness and permanence of the privilege.

So, the rebellion came and I was taken captive by rebel soldiers. They stole my possessions, they stole my privacy, and eventually they stole even my purity. And through the brutal heartbreaking experience of rape, God met with me — with outstretched arms of love." (Adapted from "The Cost of Declaring His Glory" by Helen Roseveare in *Declare His Glory Among the Nations,* edited by David M. Howard. © InterVarsity Christian Fellowship/USA. Used by permission of InterVarsity Press, P.O.Box 1400, Downers Grove, Illinois, 60515.)

We close this chapter where we began — in the arena. German theologian, Erich Sauer, describes it well for us:

"Caesar completed the arena, which was some 700 yards in length and 140 in breadth. In the time of Caesar, the number of seats is reported to have run to 150,000. (This is 50% larger than the Los Angeles Coliseum!) In Titus' time (the emperor who conquered Jerusalem in 70 A.D.) the numbers ran to 250,000! By the 300's A.D. the numbers ran to 385,000!" (*In the Arena of Faith*, Erich Sauer, Eerdmans, p.40)

Suetonius writes that Nero carried out great

gladiator shows near the camp of Mars in a wooden theater. No one was allowed to be killed during these combats, not even criminals. In his derangement, Nero required 400 senators and 600 knights to do battle in the arena. He even made some of them fight wild beasts. Nero staged a mock naval battle on an artificial salt water lake constructed for the very purpose of entertaining the Romans. Suetonius relates that "sea monsters" were swimming in it. Earlier, Claudius held a mock sea battle in the same place with 19,000 men contending in the mock battle. There were other times that Nero would drain the lake and have dinner parties there including prostitutes and dancing-girls from all over the city among his guests. (Suetonius, *The Lives of the Twelve Caesars*, p.210ff, Penguin Classics)

Sauer discusses a trip he made to the Colosseum. "Years ago we were in the Colosseum. It is the site where formerly the Golden House of Nero stood, a vast palace with many villas and gardens, fountains and lakes, and halls adorned with gold, marble and ivory. It was the scene of Nero's persecution of Christians, where shortly after Paul's time they were killed in the most horrible ways. Fifteen years after Nero, the emperors Vespasian and Titus, of the Flavian house built the vast Flavian amphitheater, the greatest example of Roman construction. The name "Colosseum" was given only later in the Middle Ages because of the nearness of a colossal statue of Nero. By night the mighty ruins rear against the sky like a specter. The most important walls, rows of seats, boxes, and doors can still be plainly recognized.

We entered the former Imperial box and gained an impressive view. We saw the box where sat the Vestal priestesses in white robes, the priestesses of the State, who had the chief decision for life or death of the defeated gladiators. We saw the great chambers with the railed cages where some 2,000 wild beasts were kept — lions, bears, elephants, giraffes, tigers and other beasts of prey from Africa and Asia. On the left was the great Door of the Living, through which passed the gladiators and martyrs to reach the arena. "Hail to thee, O Caesar: those about to die greet thee." A thousand times this had rung out before the Emperor's box. Opposite to it was the Door of Libertina, the door of the goddess of corpses, through which the fallen warriors or the dead martyrs were dragged with hooks. What a bloodthirsty ecstasy of the masses! What streams of martyr blood has flowed on this very spot in the twenty centuries from the time of the apostles. How helpless and feeble the small band of Christians then seems. How did they appear to be doomed to utter destruction without deliverance? How small one feels, especially in such a place, when remembering all those heroes, without whom we of today would not possess the treasure of the gospel.

But, what did we see in the arena, in the very center, directly in front of the ruins of the royal box? A CROSS! A plain high cross! About the year 1300 a cross was erected here in memory of the martyrs. In the course of time it was lost. In the year 1927 it was again erected by order of the Italian Government, with this most significant inscription on its base: "Ave crux spes unica," that is "Hail to thee, O Cross, the only hope!"

A Cross in the Colosseum! Exactly where formerly believers on account of their testimony to the Crucified suffered a bloody death, exactly there a cross stands erect today, bearing this so simple by mighty inscription! The seats of the heathen mockers, the walls of the Colosseum itself, lie in ruins. On the place where God's witnesses died, in the middle of the arena, stands, like a sign of triumph, a victorious, lofty cross (Ibid p.46, 47).

CHAPTER SEVEN

Follow Their Example
(Following the Leader or What Part of "Yes" Do We Not Understand?)

"Remember your leaders, those who spoke to you the word of God; consider their life, and imitate their faith."

Hebrews 13:7

I ALMOST RAN over a guy on a bicycle once. The thing is, I was so excited to have $25 — enough for a week's worth of groceries — that I just didn't see him. But, I had come across the money in a creative way; all I had to do was sell my guitar case!

If you're considering going into ministry yourself, one of the things you must realize beforehand is that you'll have to learn to make choices. Often, the right choice means doing without.

In seminary, Judy and I struggled financially, just like a lot of other students. We lived in a posh neighborhood, though, and early in the mornings, once a week, people placed their used furniture or other items out on the street to be picked up by the garbage man. More than once, Judy and I took a quick tour to "see the sights" — and see if there was anything we could use ourselves. And, like that guitar case, we sold what we could of our own belongings to raise cash. I'll never forget that antique gate-leg table that made its way out our front door one morning before dawn; we had to move quickly so our neighbors wouldn't see what we were doing.

The amazing thing was that the Lord was faithful to provide the things we really needed. One winter, we found ourselves completely out of food, as well as completely out of things we thought we could sell. We had only a half a cup of rice. But, imagine our delight when we came home from school that day to find a neighbor had come to our apartment and stocked our refrigerator while we were away! More than once, money was slipped under my door, which allowed me to buy items like toothpaste or laundry soap (I'll never know if the donors were looking for their own relief or merely sorry for my situation.)

Time and again, I found myself in Deuteronomy 8, finding comfort. In that passage, God declared He had led His people through hardship in order to do them good in the end. And it helped to keep that "end" in mind as we walked through the storms.

I have already learned that doing without shapes people in discipleship. If nothing else, it prepares us for later blessings of prosperity. Pat Robertson, for example, wrote in *Shout It From The Housetops* that in times of want in his early ministry, he sold all the furniture in his New York City apartment to give money to the poor. John Wesley, too, lived frugally in order to give, even though he generated much money throughout his lifetime.

And yet, there is tremendous blessing that comes when we say "yes" to the plan God has for our lives, and see it through even during hardship. Consider this story from *Does God Speak Today,* by David Pytches:

In his book *Signs and Wonders Today*, the Rev. Dr. Peter Wagner recounts the story of the severe drought in the city of Santa Rosa, Guatemala, in Central America. It was 1965. People were leaving the city. Businesses were going bankrupt. Crops were perishing. Animals were dying. Social efforts were made to bring water in, but it was scarce everywhere. Catholics were holding prayer meetings. There was no rain and no water.

Then it happened in a small Pentecostal meeting, where some believers from the Principe de Paz churches had assembled for their regular worship service, that the Spirit of the Lord moved in a mighty way. There was a message in tongues followed a few moments later by an interpretation. It ran like this: "Dig a well in the pastor's backyard. There you will find water." There was much opposition from other churches as the deacons, elders and pastor began to dig. They thought these people were fanatics and/or hallucinating — especially when they saw that the pastor's backyard was on a hill. A well would never be dug on a hill, as the water runs low. But the pastor, deacons and elders all continued to dig. Soon one of the deacons became quite upset.

"Why is it in the pastor's backyard? Why couldn't it be in mine?" he asked. Another elder thought that maybe the prophecy was biased. One deacon gave up. Another elder left. But there still remained a group ready to press on.

Because of the drought, the land was hard, so the digging progressed slowly. On the fourth day, they encountered a big boulder. It was so large they though they had hit solid rock. The disappointments and frustrations were intensified as another elder left the shoveling team.

But, they kept digging around the boulder until finally, after two days, they were able to remove it. As they did so, a gush of water came forth. It was rich and plenteous, and they began to drink and drink. It was a remarkable sign for the whole town. What the miracle of the well did to the growth of this church carries on until this day. The number of conversions to Christ was staggering; the entire town was influenced by it. Church membership grew from a few dozen to over nine hundred within the same year."

Of course, things don't always work out the way we want them to when we say "yes" to the Lord.. Throughout this book, you've read story after story of trials and difficulties, from Biblical times through today.

In the Book of Acts, for example, when the disciples went out and preached, they were met with religious hatred from both Jews and Gentiles. Acts 13:44-50 tells us, "When the Jews saw the multitudes, they were filled with jealousy, and contradicted what was spoken by Paul, and reviled him... The Jews incited the devout women of high standing and the leading men of the city, and stirred up persecution against Paul and Barnabas, and drove them out of the district."

In Ephesus, people were worshipping at the temple of Artemis when Paul caused a riot by preaching about Christ in the middle of the idolatrous environment. The opposition from the Gentiles was so great, in fact, that in the next chapter, we read of him moving on to Macedonia.

As for Peter and John, they were threatened by religious leaders in Jerusalem for preaching that they could only be saved through Christ. Paul faced imprisonment more than once, as seen in 2 Corinthians 11. Peter also faced imprisonment more than once. He spent many of his final days, in fact, in a Roman jail, only to be released into the hands of an executioner who crucified him upside down.

Then apostles faced phony religious and civil court proceedings, just like their forerunner, Jesus. Religious and civil opposition-to this day- seems to be part and parcel of true discipleship and cross-carrying!

Paul and Stephen, if you recall, were both stoned. Stephen died. And though there were natural disasters, they found the blessings of the Lord — and success.

On the day of Pentecost, 3,000 people were saved. Just one and a half chapters later, we read of another 5,000 added to their number. The disciples increased in number, the Jewish priests became obedient to the faith right there in Jerusalem, and the word of God increased, grew and multiplied throughout the book of Acts. The church of God was multiplied, and the gift of the Holy Spirit was poured out on many different individuals and people groups, including both Jews and Gentiles.

God raised Tabitha from the dead, and He healed Aeneas' feet. He blinded and healed the same man. And as multitudes came to know the Lord, false doctrines were overcome. All the residents of Asia heard the word of the Lord until it grew and prevailed mightily.

And, what of the trials and successes of more recent men who said "yes" to God?

Pat Robertson, the founder and president of Christian Broadcasting Network, has been lampooned by the media as being the "radical religious right" on the political scene. At the same time, hundreds and thousands of people in many countries of the world have come to a saving knowledge of Christ through one man's original obedience in starting a Christian television network. Only God knows the amount of opposition Robertson has faced — and only God knows the numbers of those blessed by his act.

Then there's Charles Colson. When Colson repented after the Watergate debacle, newspapers across the country ran cartoons portraying him as a bizarre religious fanatic carrying placards calling for the end of the world. Colson looked like a brainless wonder. Unfortunately for his detractors, however, Colson is an extremely bright and quick-minded individual. Through his obedience, literally thousands of people have been blessed, and Colson will be reaping eternal dividends for a long, long time to come.

John Calvin, the Swiss reformer, will also be reaping those dividends. His impact has been so great, in fact, that unbelieving literary critic Will Durant listed Calvin's writings as "one of 10 books that shook the world." Yet, he was never granted citizenship in his hometown of Geneva, and he was buried in an unmarked grave. The difficulties and the blessings are all too real.

For Billy Graham, the high price has been scrutiny from the press, harassment from enemies and even criticism from the saints. Yet once more, on the other side of the coin, thousands of people have been converted through his crusades, both in the United States and around the world.

So, why do we recount these stories here? Allow them to serve as a reminder for what happens when we devote ourselves fully, saying "yes" to whatever He calls us to do. The pain can be great, but the successes can be out of this world.

Conclusion:
How to Get involved in Missions

1. Give to Missions and to missionaries. Be a supporter of your churches missionaries. If your church has a missions conference, volunteer your time. Jesus said, "Where your treasure is, that is where your heart will be also."

2. Subscribe to missions magazines, journals etc. *The Evangelical Missions Quarterly* is a great place to start.

3. Let missionaries stay in your home when they are speaking in your church. This will give you and your family an "up close and personal" look at the way missionaries live —both personally and in their ministry function.

4. Pray for specific missionaries and specific nations. Peter Wagner wrote a great book titled, *The Prayer Shield* that indicates the strategic importance of praying specifically for missionaries and for nations.

5. Go on short-term missions trips with your church or with para-church organizations.

6. Ask your pastor to preach on Missions and to invite missionaries to your church to speak.

7. Read Missionary biographies. Two or three good ones to start with would be the biographies of: Amy Carmichael, Gladys Aylward or for a recent one, Jackie Pullinger.

Mission Builders International can help you do all seven of these things.

Call us at:
1-406-844-2683
Toll free from Canada and the USA:
1-866-844-2683

Email us:
MBI@MissionBuilders.net

Visit our Web Site:
www.MissionBuilders.net

Send us a letter at:
Mission Builders International
Box 406
Lakeside, Montana 59922

MISSIONS READING LIST
(Buy these books if necessary, then read them.)

1. *A Chance to Die*, Elisabeth Eliot

2. *Foxes Book of Martyrs*

3. *More Precious than Gold*, J. Christy Wilson Jr.

4. *Customs and Cultures*, Eugene Nida

5. *Guardians of the Great Commission*, Ruth Tucker

6. *A Dictionary of Women in Church History*, Mary Hammack

7. *Changing the Mind of Missions*, James F. Engel & William A. Dyrness

8. *Ministering Cross-Culturally*, Sherwood Lingenfelter & Marvin Mayers

9. *Helping Missionaries Grow*, Kelly and Michele O'Donnell

WORKING BIBLIOGRAPHY

Customs and Cultures, Eugene Nida, William Carey Library, 1705 N.Sierra Bonita Ave. P.O.Box 40129, Pasadena, California 91104.

Declare His Glory Among the Nations, edited by David Howard, IVP, Box 1400, Downers Grove, Illinois, 60515.

A Dictionary of Women in Church History, Mary L. Hammack, Moody Bible Institute, Chicago, Illinois.

Does God Speak Today?, David Pytches, Bethany House Publishers, 6820 Auto Club Road, Minneapolis, Minnesota, 55438

Eerdmans Bible Dictionary, Eerdmans Publishing Company, 225 Jefferson Ave. S.E., Grand Rapids, Michigan 49506

Guardians of the Great Commission, Ruth Tucker, Academie/Zondervan Publishers, 1415 Lake Drive S.E., Grand Rapids, Michigan 49506

Helping Missionaries Grow, Kelly and Michele O'Donnell, William Carey Library, P.O.Box 40129, Pasadena, California, 91114

In The Arena of Faith, Erich Sauer, Eerdmans Publishing Company, 225 Jefferson Ave., S.E., Grand Rapids, Michigan 49503

Persecution and Martyrdom in the Theology of Paul, John S. Pobee, Sheffield Press, University of Sheffield, Sheffield S10 2TN, England

Perspectives on the World Christian Movement, (3rd Edition), edited by Ralph Winter and Stephen Hawthorne, William Carey Library, P.O.Box 40129, Pasadena, California, 91114

Through Five Hundred Years, Allen W. Schattschneider, The Moravian Church in America, P.O.Box 1245, Bethlehem, Pennsylvania, 18016-1245

Tortured for Christ, Richard Wurmbrand, Living Sacrifice Books, P.O.Box 2273, Bartlesville, Oklahoma 74005-2273. Published by The Voice of the Martyrs, 800-747-0085, www.persecution.com

Vicars of Christ, Peter de Rosa, Crown Publishers, New York.

Epilogue
From Mission Builders International

MISSION BUILDERS INTERNATIONAL (MBI) is pleased to sponsor and publish *Under the Mosquito Net (an Inside Look at Missions.)*

Imagine the different outcome had someone been there to lift the arms of many of the missionaries mentioned in this book. Imagine enabling a missionary or someone in need to know the love of Jesus in a practical way. Your simple obedience to responding to the heart of God can be life changing. *You* could be a missionary's miracle in the next few months and years by just showing up: to bring encouragement, renewed hope and strength through servant-hearted, practical work.

The stories, statistics and samples from the lives of missionaries around the world represent what MBI is about: mobilizing Christians worldwide into active service, equipping them to encourage, support and work alongside front-line missionaries to build the Kingdom of God; to provide ministry and facility development services that promote health, education and economic opportunities for hurting people.

Will you come with us? You don't have to go to the most difficult places first. We'll help you get started by giving you practical steps to turn your life-successes into significance.

Where do you start? Pray first! Then contact us through the worldwide web at www.Mission-Builders.net Enter your personal profile of information so we can match your gifts, talents and interests with the ministries needing your help. If you don't have Internet access, call us toll free at 1-866-844-2683.

Every ministry and every missionary is different from one another; and every Mission Builder volunteer is unique as well. Only you can bring the gifts and skills God has entrusted to you to build the Kingdom. God doesn't waste His resources: your talents have a place in the Body of Christ, let Mission

Builders International help you find where to put them to use.

There's a place for everyone with a heart to serve and a willingness to go and discover how God can use them!

Now, let us hear from you. May God give you peace as you pursue His Presence.

In Jesus' Name,

John Briggs
President/CEO

Mission Builders International
PO Box 406
Lakeside, MT 59922 USA
Phone: 1-406-844-2683
Email: MBI@MissionBuilders.net